The Middle School Student's Guide to Ruling the World!*

D0817465

* Through Work Management and Organizational Skills

This book belongs to:

_____

www.middleschoolguide.com

ISBN 0-9785210-0-5

TABLE OF CONTENTS

Welcome to The Middle School Student's Guide to Ruling the World!

The First Stop: The Middle School Tool Shed

Middle School Confidential:
Students *Only!*

CONFIDENTIAL

Middle School Confidential:
Students Only!

Welcome to *The Middle School Student's Guide to Ruling the World!* This book is not for your teacher and it's not for your parents. It was written *just* for you: the middle school (or soon-to-be middle school) student. Sorry, but this book won't help you dominate the middle school social scene, or deal with bullies or queen bees. What it *will do* is teach you how to successfully organize and manage your middle school workload. It is a practical, and sometimes fun, introduction to the basic work management and organizational skills you'll need to do well in middle school.

Why take the time or make the effort to learn how to manage and organize your school work? Let's see... do better grades sound good? How about less stress? More free time? More self-confidence? These are all benefits of a well-managed school workload and if any sound good to you, read on!

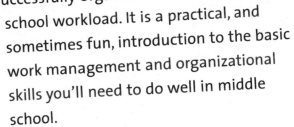

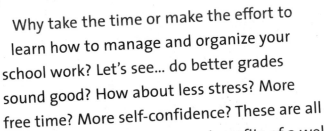

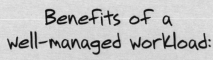

Benefits of a well-managed workload:
- ✓ Less stress
- ✓ Better grades
- ✓ More self-confidence
- ✓ More Free Time

Some Good News and Some Bad News...

Congratulations! You've either made it to middle school or you're on your way! There's some good news and some bad news about middle school. The good news is, you're growing up and moving up! Middle school is the last stop before high school. In middle school, you'll make new friends, enjoy new activities and have more independence than you had in elementary school.

What's the bad news? Middle school is harder now than ever. Classes are larger and subjects are more complex. Even bright students, who sailed through elementary school, are often surprised to discover that in middle school, the workload can be overwhelming.

How can that be? What's so different about middle school? In middle school, students have many different teachers, each with different homework and test schedules, and different expectations of their students. Assignments must be completed and turned in on time. Students are expected to keep up with assigned reading, and contribute to the class discussion every day. There are after-school clubs, activities and sports practices. There's a lot to keep track of and many demands on a student's time. In middle school, students often underachieve because of poor work management and organizational skills.

Is there any more good news? There's plenty of good news. You're young! You're not yet in high school where grades begin to count toward college admission. As a middle school student, you have the time and the opportunity to develop good work management and organizational skills. Such skills will serve you well over the coming years, and can make your life a lot easier now.

Are work management and organizational skills hard to learn? No! Good work management and organizational skills are easy to learn—even for a chronically disorganized student. In fact, you may not believe this now, but it is actually much harder and more stressful to be *dis*organized than it is to be organized.

Where can these skills be learned? Right here in *The Middle School Student's Guide to Ruling the World*! C'mon! Follow along with the students of U.B. Smart Middle School as they take a journey to success in middle school!

NEWSFLASH!

Scandal Rocks Ms. Readmore's Class!

By R.E. PORTER

Shocking news from U.B. Smart Middle School! Five organizationally-challenged students have been discovered in Ms. Readmore's 3rd period Language Arts class.

These chronically disorganized kids lack basic work management and organizational skills. Ms. Readmore was able to identify the students by their late and missing assignments, disastrous binder conditions, empty planners, overdue library books and general confusion about school. Study the picture on page 9. Can you find them? Circle the students you see making work management and organizational errors. Then, describe their errors in the space provided.

> **HINT!**
> **There are more than 10 errors in the picture.**

Describe the Students' Errors:

_____

_____

_____

_____

_____

_____

_____

_____

_____

_____

_____

_____

How did you do? Check your answers on pages 10 and 11.

Meet the ORGANIZATIONALLY-CHALLENGED Students of U.B. Smart Middle School

Meet Chronically Disorganized Chris. On the outside he's cool, he's popular, he's laid back. On the inside, he's a bundle of nerves. His parents are always on him about his grades and think he's a slacker. He barely keeps up with homework. He forgot his language arts book at home, so he brought his math book to class instead, hoping Ms. Readmore won't notice. (She will.) His planner is open, but nothing's written in it. This is not unusual for Chris. Some of his teachers think his head is as empty as his planner, but don't be too sure! *Chris's errors: forgetting his book at home, not using his planner, missing assignments.*

This is Scattered Sara. She's bright, but just can't seem to get organized. What are Sara's errors? Check it out: While Ms. Readmore is instructing the class about Wednesday's test, she's busy chatting with her friend Polly. She's written down the wrong date for the test, and hasn't listened to anything her teacher's said. She's lost so many worksheets, assignments and permission slips, she's beginning to think her backpack is a mysterious vortex, sucking her papers into another dimension. *Sara's errors: lost permission slip, wrong test date in planner, messy binder and backpack, distracted in class.*

Late Larry. Obviously, Larry is late for class. That might have something to do with the fact that his watch says it's 10:00, but the actual time is 10:10. Last night he stayed up too late finishing his homework which, incidentally, has fallen out of his backpack. Five missing assignments have brought his grade in the class down to a D. Between football practice and flirting with cheerleaders, Larry thinks he has no time to get organized. As he approaches the classroom door he's working on the excuses he'll give Ms. Readmore when she asks why he's late to class (again) and where his homework is (again).
Larry's errors: tardies, missing assignments, disastrous backpack conditions, lost homework, nasty homework habits.

Larry

Say hello to Perfect Polly. Her hair is perfect. Her clothes are perfect. She always looks super organized—like she's got everything under control. But Polly has a dirty little secret: She's a fake, a total poser. She's totally dependent on her mother to keep track of her assignments and responsibilities. Her mom even edits her papers! Polly desperately wants to be more independent, but she's terrified that without her mother's "help," she'll crash and burn in one semester. Polly doesn't know it, but her mother has a secret too: She'd like Polly to grow up and be more responsible.
Polly's errors: overdue library books, relying on others to keep track of her responsibilities (check out the reminder notes from Mom) and being so distracted in class that she's missed out on directions about the test.

Polly

This is Jamal. He is shy and quiet. He rarely talks to teachers and doesn't participate much in class. Although his grades are mostly average, Jamal is not at all an average student. He's a total brainiac, but his abilities are hidden by his messy and misspelled work. Today Jamal is disappointed because he received a low grade on his paper. Why? Because it contains misspelled words, punctuation errors and boring vocabulary. Unfortunately, Ms. Readmore can't recognize the talents of this unassuming middle school genius because she can't see past the mess and mistakes! The problem is, Jamal is too shy to ask for help!
Jamal's errors: poor quality written work; failing to ask for help; not participating in class.

Jamal

The Journey Begins with a Mysterious Map

The bell rings and Ms. Readmore dismisses her class. She asks Chris, Sara, Polly, Jamal and Larry to stay a few minutes longer. When the room clears, she gathers the five disorganized students around her desk. She tells them that she is concerned because, although they are bright and caring students, their lack of work management and organizational skills are holding them back from achieving the success they deserve in middle school. Ms. Readmore explains that with good work management and organizational skills, they will get better grades, have more self-confidence, and maybe even have more free time to do the things they really like to do!

Ms. Readmore takes a key from her pocket, opens the top drawer of her desk and removes a neatly rolled document. She opens it up and places it on her desk. Curious, the students draw nearer. To their surprise, it's a map! But this map is unlike any map they have ever seen. At the top is U.B. Smart Middle School, but they've never heard of the other places—The Middle School Tool Shed, The Homework Detective Agency and Motivation Mountain.

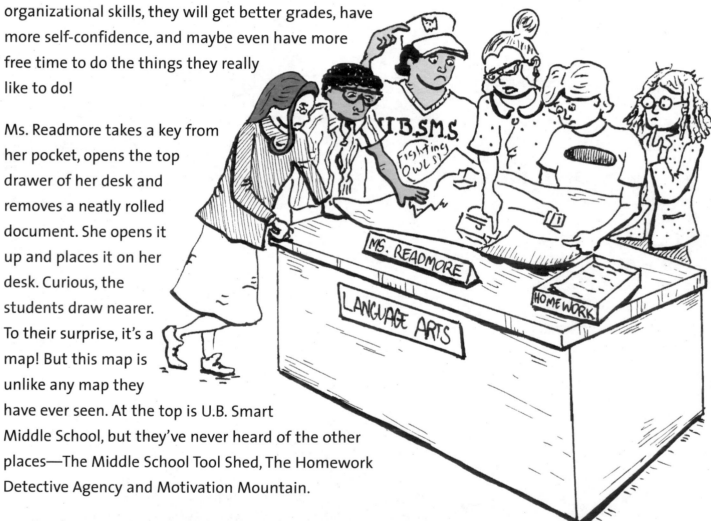

Ms. Readmore explains that she has a special assignment for them. She is sending them on a journey. It is a journey to success in middle school. They are to follow the map and along the way, discover the work management and organizational skills they need for success in middle school and beyond!

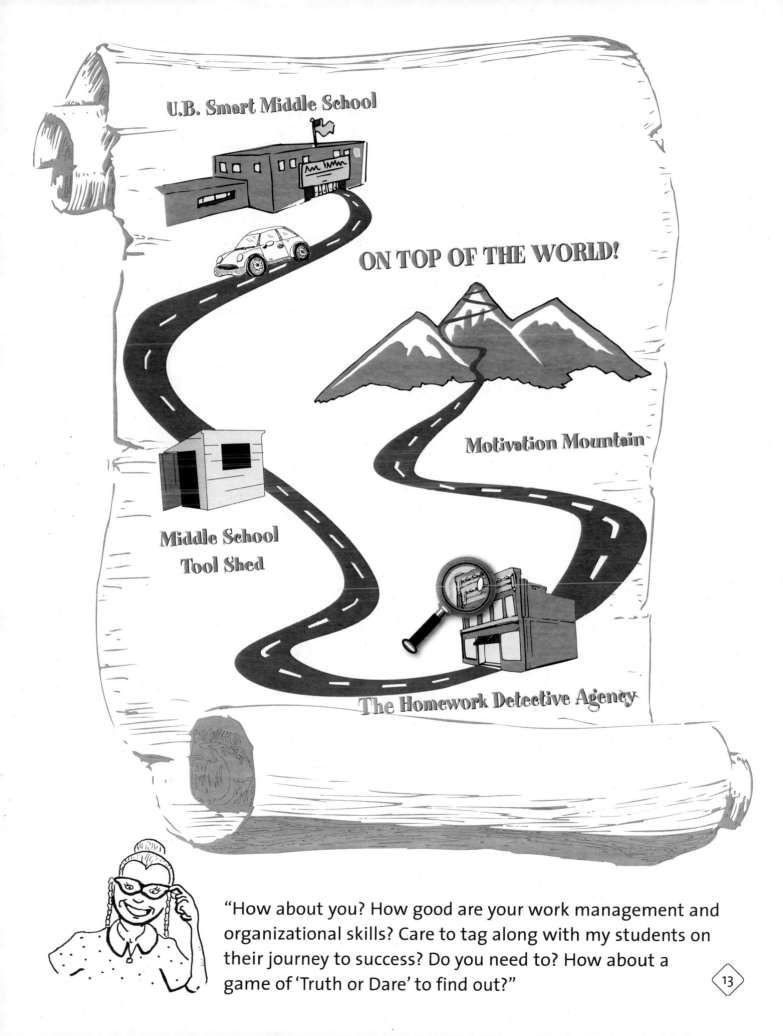

U.B. Smart Middle School

ON TOP OF THE WORLD!

Motivation Mountain

Middle School
Tool Shed

The Homework Detective Agency

"How about you? How good are your work management and organizational skills? Care to tag along with my students on their journey to success? Do you need to? How about a game of 'Truth or Dare' to find out?"

How do you rate your skills? Truth?

Are you like Chronically Disorganized Chris? Are you more like Scattered Sara or Late Larry? Maybe you're like Polly who depends too much on others to keep track of her responsibilites, or Jamal, whose genius is masked by his messy work. Take this quiz (if you *dare!*) Find out the *truth* about your work management and organizational skills!

5 = Absolutely, always!   4 = Well, almost always!   3 = Sometimes...
2 = Hardly ever!   1 = No, Never!

	Always!	Almost always	Sometimes	Hardly ever	Never
My binder is organized by class and the contents are easy to find.	5	4	3	2	1
My essays, reports and written work are neat, with no spelling or punctuation errors.	5	4	3	2	1
I do my homework in a quiet, private place.	5	4	3	2	1
My homework space is stocked with all the homework supplies I need.	5	4	3	2	1
I have a reliable friend in each of my classes whom I contact when I have a question about an assignment and I have their phone number in my binder.	5	4	3	2	1
I use a thesaurus when I write papers and essays.	5	4	3	2	1
I know of helpful homework websites for every subject I am studying.	5	4	3	2	1
In class, I listen carefully for information about homework assignments or projects and I write the information in my planner right away.	5	4	3	2	1
I check my school's website at least twice a week.	5	4	3	2	1
I remember all of the things I need to bring to school each day (like homework, books, permission slips, lunch or lunch money,) without having to be reminded by a parent or other grown up.	5	4	3	2	1
I read and carefully follow the rubric or other directions my teacher gives me for assignments or projects.	5	4	3	2	1
I feel comfortable asking any of my teachers for help.	5	4	3	2	1
I have an assignment calendaring system and I use it every day.	5	4	3	2	1
My assignments are completed and turned in on time.	5	4	3	2	1
I accurately keyboard at least 20 to 25 words per minute.	5	4	3	2	1

Your Truth score: __ + __ + __ + __ + __ =

or Dare!

WARNING!

The scoring key changes for these questions:

1 = Absolutely, always! 2 = Well, almost always! 3 = Sometimes...
4 = Hardly ever! 5 = No, Never!

	Always!	Almost always	Sometimes	Hardly ever	Never
My parents are not satisfied with my grades.	1	2	3	4	5
Fear of being in trouble with my parents or teacher motivates me to get my school work done!	1	2	3	4	5
I forget about test or quiz dates.	1	2	3	4	5
I don't work as hard at subjects I'm not good in.	1	2	3	4	5
With regard to finishing projects, I am the king/queen of the last minute rush!	1	2	3	4	5
I put off doing my homework for as long as possible.	1	2	3	4	5
I have missing assignments.	1	2	3	4	5
I dread working on group projects.	1	2	3	4	5
I misplace papers, packets, worksheets or other materials my teacher provides for me.	1	2	3	4	5
I rely on my mom, dad or other adult to keep track of my schedule.	1	2	3	4	5
I listen to music, watch t.v. or talk to others as I do homework.	1	2	3	4	5
I have gotten so frustrated over homework or a school project that I have cried, yelled or pitched a fit.	1	2	3	4	5
My mom, dad or other adult has gotten so frustrated with me over my homework or a school project that they have cried, yelled or pitched a fit.	1	2	3	4	5
I hope my teacher won't call on me in class.	1	2	3	4	5
I put papers loose into my backpack or locker.	1	2	3	4	5

Your Dare score: __ + __ + __ + __ + __ =

Truth Score [ ] **+ Dare Score** [ ] **= [ ]**

Check your organizational profile on the next page → → →

If you scored between 130 and 150

Congratulations! You are a motivated student and have developed excellent organizational skills at a young age. Unlike Polly, you handle your schedule, responsibilities and workload independently. You do not rely on your mom, dad or other adult for help. Your assignments are never late. Your papers are perfect. You use your planner like a pro. You're totally awesome! Are you for *real?*

If you scored between 100 and 129

Not bad! Your work management and organizational system could use a boost, but so far you've kept out of trouble. You depend a little too much on a parent or other grown up to remind you of your responsibilities and to keep track of your schedule. You don't use your planner consistently, but know that you should. Like Sara, you probably socialize in class, sometimes missing out on what your teacher says. You occasionally stay up late to finish homework or to complete a project. You worry that when the work load increases, you may not have the skills to manage it.

If you scored between 64 and 99

Hmm... your work management and organizational skills are definitely on the slim side. You're a capable student but, like Jamal, your talents are often masked by the poor or rushed quality of your work. Like Larry, you may have missing assignments, or turn in homework late, which drags down your grade. You don't use your planner much, and your binder and backpack are a mess. You're distracted by things that are more interesting than school (who isn't?). Your parents think you're not trying hard enough. You *do* try, but you just can't seem to stay on top of all the work!

If you scored between 30 and 63

Whoa! You've got a lot in common with Chris. You look cool, but you're living on the edge! Your binders are a mess—your locker and backpack are too. You complete assignments at the last minute. You don't participate much in class because you're afraid that your answers will reveal to the teacher how little studying or reading you've actually done. You're a smart kid, but you'd never know it by the grades you've been getting! You sometimes forget to bring your homework to school and without help, have trouble seeing projects through to the end. You're tired of your parents and teachers nagging at you about your work habits and grades. Guess what? They're tired of it too!

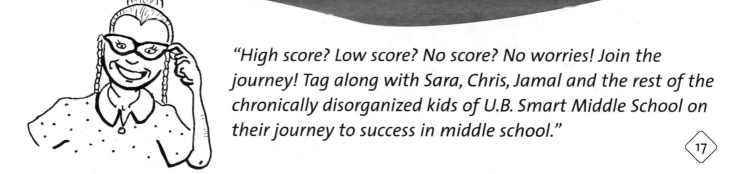

"High score? Low score? No score? No worries! Join the journey! Tag along with Sara, Chris, Jamal and the rest of the chronically disorganized kids of U.B. Smart Middle School on their journey to success in middle school."

Notes:

STOP

**FIRST STOP:
THE MIDDLE
SCHOOL TOOL SHED!**

The Middle School Tool Shed

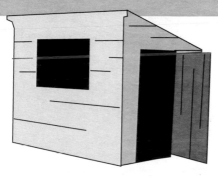

Welcome to the Middle School Tool Shed, the first stop on the journey to success in middle school. Everyone knows that to do a good job, you need to use the right tools. Having the right tools and using them correctly, makes any job easier.

Did you know that there are tools for middle school students? Not hammers or saws, but tools to help them manage and organize their school work.

Step inside the Middle School Tool Shed and discover the 10 tools every student needs to succeed!

Tool Number 1:
The Binder

The journey to success in middle school starts with an organized binder. An organized binder is a valuable tool for saving time and keeping track of your school work. Think of your binder as sort of a compact file cabinet that you carry around all day to file and retrieve handouts, notes, information and homework. The goal is to create a system that lets you file papers in an organized way, so that they can be easily located and quickly retrieved. Whether school has just started, or you're in the middle of a school year, take the time to organize your binder into a "Goof-Proof™" system!

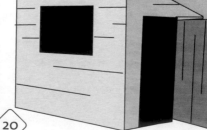

SCATTERED SARA IS SO SICK OF NEVER BEING ABLE TO FIND HER PAPERS, HANDOUTS AND HOMEWORK. LAST WEEK SHE HANDED IN HER MATH HOMEWORK IN SCIENCE AND LOST HER PERMISSION SLIP FOR THE FIELD TRIP TO THE CHEESE FACTORY. SARA'S DECIDED ENOUGH IS ENOUGH! SHE'S DETERMINED TO SET UP A SYSTEM WHERE SHE CAN QUICKLY FIND, FILE AND KEEP TRACK OF ALL HER IMPORTANT PAPERS.

SCATTERED SARA DESIGNS A
GOOF-PROOF BINDER SYSTEM

Poor Scattered Sara, always searching for assignments, homework and handouts! She's decided that it's time to get her binder organized. For obvious reasons, the file-cabinet approach wasn't practical. After visiting the Middle School Tool Shed, Sara designed a binder system that's easy to use and lets her store, organize and retrieve her papers quickly. In this chapter, Sara shares the secret of her Goof-Proof Binder System with you.

Sara's Goof-Proof Binder System

"OK everybody, listen up! In middle school it's important to have an organized binder. An organized binder helps you keep papers filed in the right place, so they won't get lost. It also helps you find important information fast, like class schedules, study guides and reading lists. Believe me, having an organized binder makes middle school life a lot easier!

CAUTION!

"**Most teachers let students decide for themselves what kind of binders to use and how to organize them. But some schools or teachers have specific rules about binders. So, if your teacher gives you instructions for organizing a class binder, follow them carefully!**"

Binder Styles

There are many different binder styles and sizes. The capacity of a binder (that means how much stuff it will hold) is determined by the size of the binder rings. Rings for school binders can be anywhere from one half inch (1/2") to three inches (3"). Some binders fasten with Velcro, others zip. Some come with pockets, some with pencil bags. With so many choices, it should be easy to find a binder style that's right for you. Here's how:

Sara's having a bad hair day

Standard Style vs. Notebook Style

A *standard style binder* is a three-ring, vinyl binder. They come in all sizes and colors. A standard binder with 1/2" to 1" rings is just right for holding materials for one class. If you want to put materials for more than one class in a standard binder, look for one with rings that are 1.5" or larger.

A *notebook style binder* has three rings, a larger capacity and can easily hold materials for more than one class. The exterior of the binder is made of a water resistant material and it closes by zipper or Velcro. Some come with built in pockets and pencil bags.

How Many Binders Will You Need?

After deciding what style of binder is best for you, figure out how many you'll need. To do this, make a list of your middle school classes. Include activities you're involved in like clubs, band or the school play. Circle "a.m." if it's a morning class, and "p.m." if it's an afternoon class.

Here's my list of classes and activities

1. History	am/**pm**
2. Language Arts	**am**/pm
3. Drama	**am**/pm
4. Science	am/**pm**
5. Math	am/**pm**
6. Tech	**am**/pm
7. Band	am/**pm**

1.	am/pm
2.	am/pm
3.	am/pm
4.	am/pm
5.	am/pm
6.	am/pm
7.	am/pm

Make YOUR list of classes and activities here.

OK, Now Count up Your Classes!

If you plan to use a separate binder for each class and activity, you'll need *one* binder for *each* class and activity on your list. Try using a different color for each class and activity. That will help you tell your binders apart when you're in a rush!

If you plan to put materials for more than one class in your binder, try using one binder for morning classes and another binder for afternoon classes. Use a standard binder for after-school activities, like the band or the school play.

I use two notebook style binders. One holds the materials for my three morning classes. The other holds materials for my afternoon classes. At lunch break, I go to my locker and switch binders!

First Stop: The Middle School Tool Shed

Now let's get the inside of your binder organized!

What goes inside your binder to make it Goof-Proof?

Binder inserts (also called binder accessories) are an important part of the Goof-Proof Binder System. Whatever style of binder you choose to use, these inserts will help keep the inside of your binder organized!

1. Subject dividers.

Always keep papers, handouts and homework separated by *class*. Science handouts belong in the science section of your binder, math papers belong in the math section—you get it. **Subject dividers** are great, because they make it easy to keep materials separated by class. Plastic subject dividers are best because they won't rip or tear, and fall out of your binder.

2. Plastic sheet protectors.

Sheet protectors are cool because they preserve and protect all of your important class handouts. Always use sheet protectors to hold things like your class schedule, course syllabus, class rules and expectations, reading lists, supply lists, rubrics, grading policies and grade logs—stuff you have to keep in your binder to refer to during the school year.

3. Binder paper.

Most middle schools require students to use **wide-ruled binder paper**. Any brand will do. (Some math teachers want students to use graph paper. Check with your math teacher about that.)

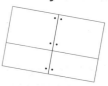

4. Two-pocket folder.

A three hole-punched, **2-pocket folder** is great for holding worksheets, handouts and homework—stuff you have to move in and out of your binder each day. Poly Pocket folders are made of a plastic-like material and are best because they won't rip or tear and fall out of your binder.

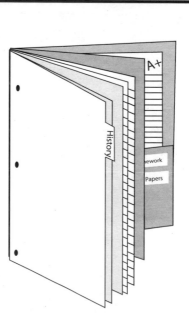

Write your name here

_____ 's

Goof-Proof BINDER SHOPPING LIST ✔ Got It!

1. Standard vinyl or notebook style binders.

How many? _____

2. Plastic subject dividers.

One (1) plastic three hole-punched subject divider (with tab labels) for **each** class and activity on your list. (You'll need about 7 or 8 of these.)

3. Plastic sheet protectors.

Clear, top-loading standard weight sheet protectors. (You'll need 50 or more of these!)

4. Binder paper.

Wide-ruled. Buy extra binder paper to store in your desk at home. If you use graph paper for math, be sure to buy some.

5. Plastic pocket folder.

A 2-pocket, three-hole punched (Poly Pocket) folder for **each** class and activity on your list.

6. One permanent marker (black) or a label maker.

Here's a **Goof-Proof Binder Shopping List** that you can copy and use when you shop for your Goof-Proof Binder!

You can also go to: www.middleschoolguide.com to download and print this form!

Putting It All Together!

You're doing great! Once you've got your binders and binder inserts, you're good to go. Just follow these easy steps to assemble your very own Goof-Proof Binder!

Step 1

Find a large space to work in, like the kitchen table or living room floor. Place one binder in front of you and open it up.

Step 2

Take one plastic subject divider and, starting with the first class or activity on your "Class and Activity List," use the permanent marker (or label maker) to label the tab of the subject divider with the name of the class or activity.

Step 3

Place the labeled plastic subject divider into your binder, laying to the left side.

Step 4

Place five or six plastic sheet protectors behind the subject divider. Sheet protectors hold class handouts that you'll need to use or refer to throughout the school year, such as the **class schedule**, **syllabus**, **rules**, **project rubrics** and **reading lists**. If your teacher gives you a multiple page handout that has been stapled together, pull it apart and place each page in a sheet protector so each page can be seen. As you receive updated handouts, remove the old ones and replace them with the new ones.

Step 5

Place 20–25 sheets of binder paper (or graph paper in the case of math) behind the sheet protectors. The binder paper is for **homework**, **class notes**, **in-class assignments**, **tests** and **quizzes**. Refill binder paper as needed.

Step 6

Place a 2-pocket folder behind the binder paper section. Open it up. Label the left side of the pocket folder "Handouts & Worksheets." Label the right side "Homework/Graded Papers/Signed Forms." The left pocket holds **regular class handouts** like **worksheets and study guides**. The right pocket holds your **finished homework**, **graded papers** and **forms that need to be signed and returned to school**. Always place your homework in the right pocket when you finish it. Remove graded papers and store them at home.

Step 7

Repeat Steps 2–6 for each class and activity on your Class and Activity list.

When assembled, a subject section of your binder should look like this:

20–25 sheets of wide-ruled binder paper (or graph paper for math).

2-pocket folder with the right pocket for homework, graded papers and forms that need to be signed and returned to school. The left pocket holds handouts and worksheets.

Ta DAAAA!!

Plastic subject divider with the tab labeled with the name of the class or activity.

Sheet protectors to hold important class handouts that you need to refer to throughout the school year.

BUST THAT CLUTTER!

Binders that are stuffed with old papers and handouts won't be Goof-Proof for long, so bust that clutter! Toss out papers you don't need. Store graded papers, notes and old handouts at home.

 YOUR BACKPACK IS NOT YOUR BINDER!

Papers belong in your binder, *never* shoved loose into your backpack! With the Goof-Proof Binder System, it takes only a few seconds to file papers in the right place. If you don't have time to file papers in class, keep an extra 2-pocket folder in your backpack. Use it to *temporarily* hold papers and handouts until you have time to file them in your binder.

DITTO FOR YOUR LOCKER!

 Papers that are tossed into your locker will end up lost or squished at the bottom, along with last week's moldy cheese sandwich. If you can't resist tossing papers into your locker, buy a magnetic filing pocket (available at office supply stores). Place it on the inside of your locker door. Use it to *temporarily* hold papers and handouts until you have the time to file them in your binder.

Let's Practice Middle School Work Management and Organizational Skills!

The Goof-Proof Binder

1. An organized binder is important because it helps you:

    a. keep papers filed in the right place, so they won't get lost.

    b. find important information fast.

    c. store, organize and retrieve papers, homework and handouts quickly.

    d. all of the above.

2. A notebook style binder:

    a. has a large capacity to hold materials for more than one class.

    b. closes with a zipper or Velcro.

    c. has a water resistant exterior.

    d. all of the above.

3. Your science teacher has given the class instructions for organizing their science binders. You:

    a. ignore her directions and organize your science binder the way you want.

    b. tell her that you have a better, goof-proof method.

    c. carefully follow your science teacher's instructions.

    d. none of the above.

4. Always use plastic sheet protectors to preserve and protect important papers and class handouts, such as:

    a. class schedules, reading lists and supply lists.

    b. rubrics, grading policies and grade logs.

    c. any paper or handout you may need to refer to for any extended period of time.

    d. all of the above

5. Always keep papers, handouts and homework separated by:

    a. day.

    b. alphabetical order.

    c. class.

    d. none of the above.

6. Which of these sandwiches is most frequently found squished and moldy at the bottom of a middle school locker?

    a. bologna

    b. cheese

    c. peanut better and jelly

    d. I won't answer such a silly question!

7. If you use single subject binders, you will need _____ binder(s) for each class and activity.

    a. one

    b. two

    c. three

    d. three hundred

8. Papers should _____ be shoved loose into your backpack or locker!

    a. always

    b. never

    c. sometimes

    d. none of the above

9. True or false? You can go to www.middleschoolguide.com to download and print as many Goof-Proof Binder Shopping Lists as you need.

    a. True

    b. False

10. Select the correct order of binder inserts to assemble a Goof-Proof Binder:

    a. binder paper, subject divider, 2-pocket folder, sheet protectors.

    b. subject divider, sheet protectors, binder paper, 2-pocket folder.

    c. subject divider, 2-pocket folder, sheet protectors, binder paper.

    d. sheet protectors, subject divider, 2-pocket folder, binder paper.

How did you do? Check your answers on page 169.

Notes:

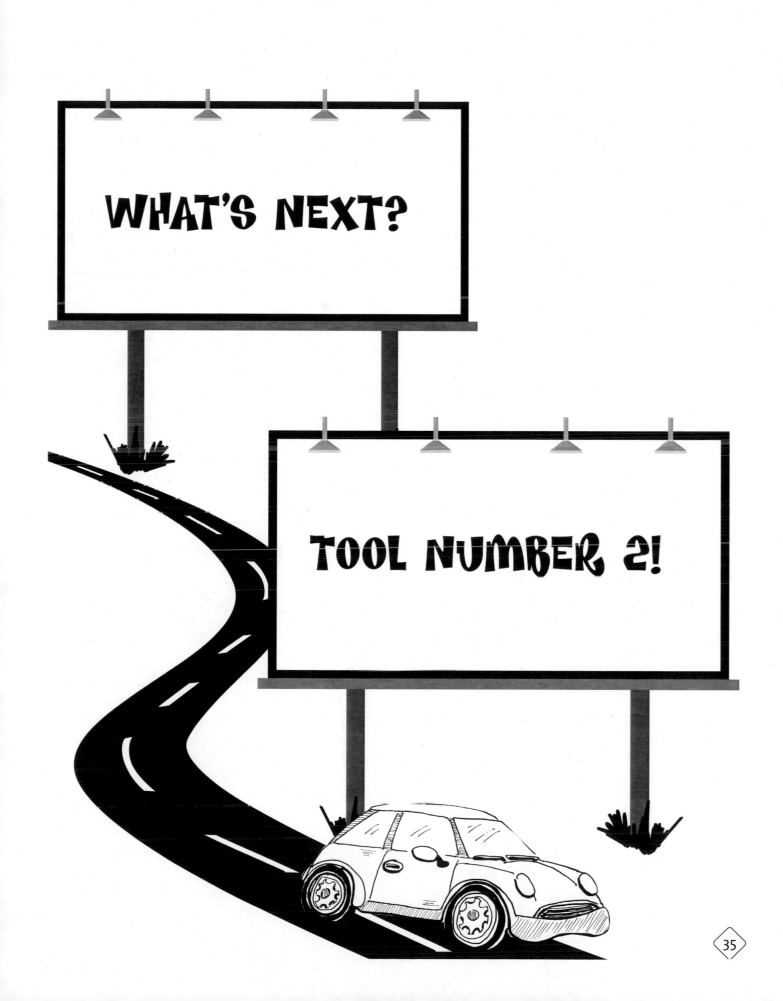

Tool Number 2:
The Planner

Most middle schools encourage students to use a daily planner or calendaring system to keep track of assignments, projects and activities. The problem is, some students don't use a planner because they think it's too hard to use, too much trouble or not worth the effort. But, used correctly and consistently, a planner is a valuable tool to help middle school students stay organized and manage their workload. Check it out. Learning to use a planner is as easy as 1-2-3!

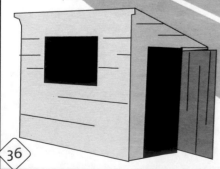

CHRONICALLY DISORGANIZED CHRIS GETS HELP FOR A CASE OF "PPD" (PERSONAL PLANNER DISORDER)

Chris owns a planner. Sometimes he carries it around with him. Once in a while he opens it and stares at its blank pages. Last semester, he actually *wrote* in it—twice. Lately, Chris has begun to suspect that there may be a benefit to using his planner on a daily basis. Uncertain about how, when or why to use a planner, he has sought the advice of the world-famous planner expert, Dear Blabby.

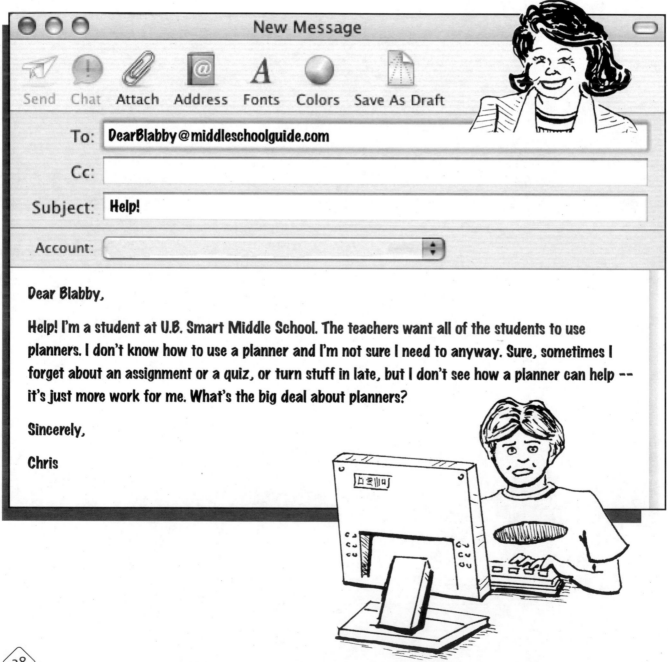

New Message

Send   Chat   Attach   Address   Fonts   Colors   Save As Draft

To: DearBlabby@middleschoolguide.com

Cc:

Subject: Help!

Account:

Dear Blabby,

Help! I'm a student at U.B. Smart Middle School. The teachers want all of the students to use planners. I don't know how to use a planner and I'm not sure I need to anyway. Sure, sometimes I forget about an assignment or a quiz, or turn stuff in late, but I don't see how a planner can help -- it's just more work for me. What's the big deal about planners?

Sincerely,

Chris

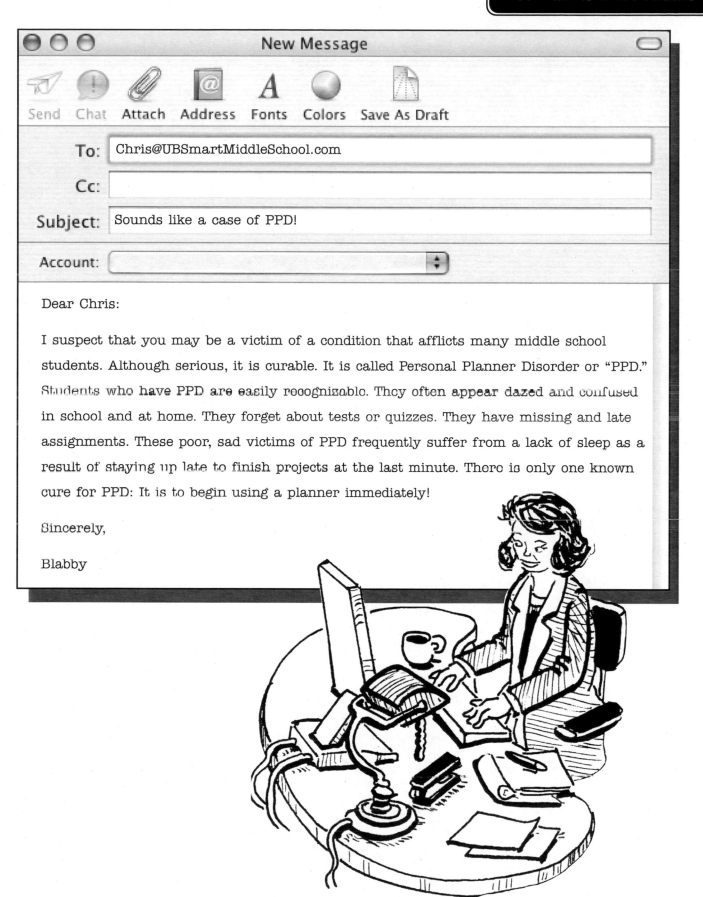

New Message

Send   Chat   Attach   Address   Fonts   Colors   Save As Draft

To: Chris@UBSmartMiddleSchool.com

Cc:

Subject: Sounds like a case of PPD!

Account:

Dear Chris:

I suspect that you may be a victim of a condition that afflicts many middle school students. Although serious, it is curable. It is called Personal Planner Disorder or "PPD." Students who have PPD are easily recognizable. They often appear dazed and confused in school and at home. They forget about tests or quizzes. They have missing and late assignments. These poor, sad victims of PPD frequently suffer from a lack of sleep as a result of staying up late to finish projects at the last minute. There is only one known cure for PPD: It is to begin using a planner immediately!

Sincerely,

Blabby

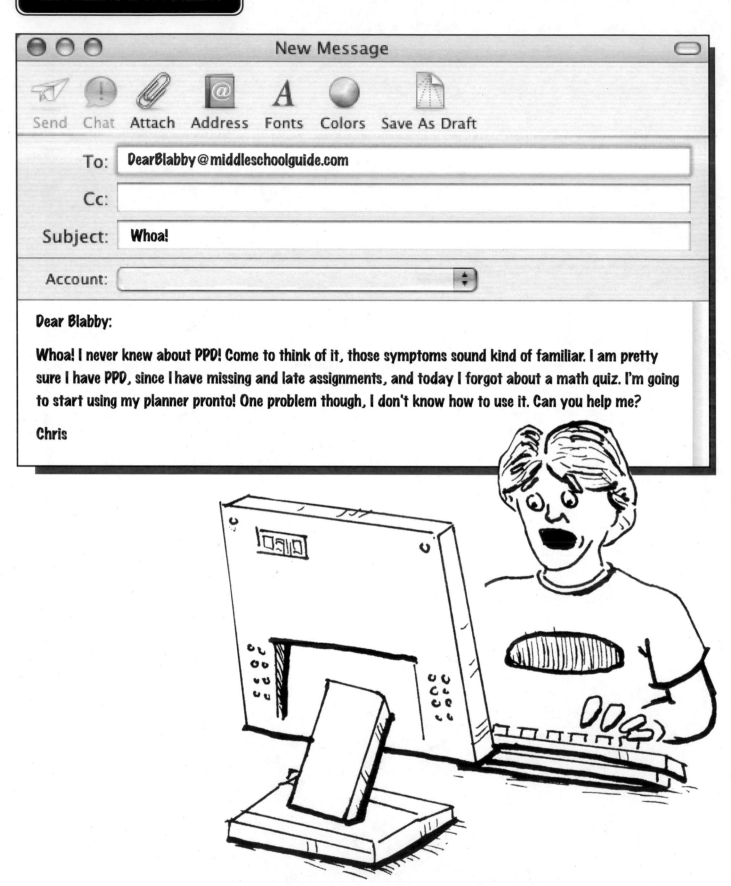

New Message

Send   Chat   Attach   Address   Fonts   Colors   Save As Draft

To: DearBlabby@middleschoolguide.com

Cc:

Subject: Whoa!

Account:

Dear Blabby:

Whoa! I never knew about PPD! Come to think of it, those symptoms sound kind of familiar. I am pretty sure I have PPD, since I have missing and late assignments, and today I forgot about a math quiz. I'm going to start using my planner pronto! One problem though, I don't know how to use it. Can you help me?

Chris

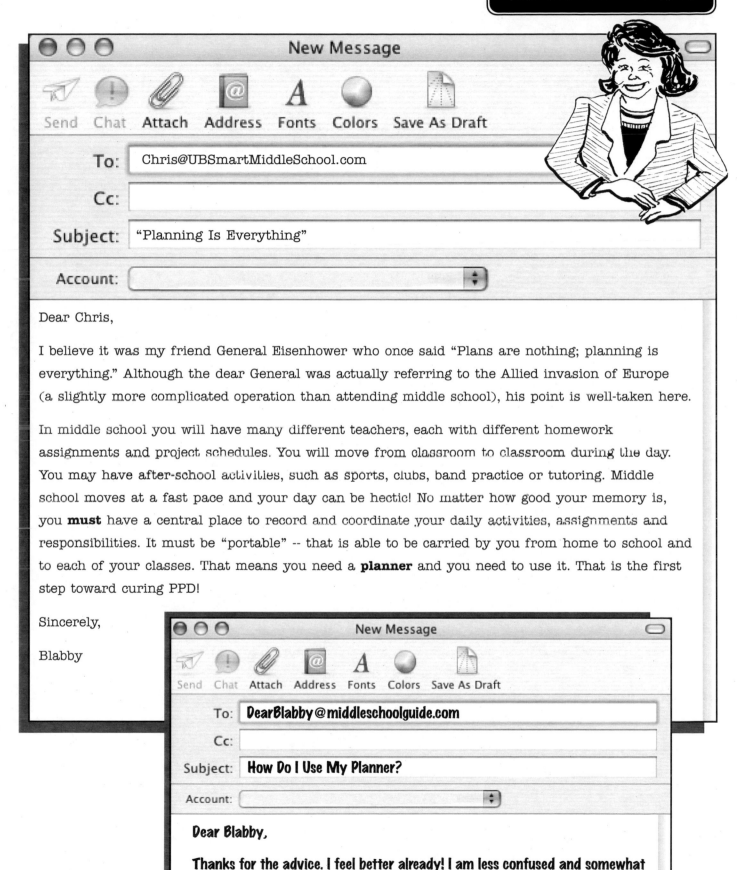

New Message

Send | Chat | Attach | Address | Fonts | Colors | Save As Draft

To: Chris@UBSmartMiddleSchool.com

Cc:

Subject: "Planning Is Everything"

Account:

Dear Chris,

I believe it was my friend General Eisenhower who once said "Plans are nothing; planning is everything." Although the dear General was actually referring to the Allied invasion of Europe (a slightly more complicated operation than attending middle school), his point is well-taken here.

In middle school you will have many different teachers, each with different homework assignments and project schedules. You will move from classroom to classroom during the day. You may have after-school activities, such as sports, clubs, band practice or tutoring. Middle school moves at a fast pace and your day can be hectic! No matter how good your memory is, you **must** have a central place to record and coordinate your daily activities, assignments and responsibilities. It must be "portable" -- that is able to be carried by you from home to school and to each of your classes. That means you need a **planner** and you need to use it. That is the first step toward curing PPD!

Sincerely,

Blabby

New Message

Send | Chat | Attach | Address | Fonts | Colors | Save As Draft

To: DearBlabby@middleschoolguide.com

Cc:

Subject: How Do I Use My Planner?

Account:

Dear Blabby,

Thanks for the advice. I feel better already! I am less confused and somewhat hopeful. But what information do I write in my planner? How do I use it?

Chris

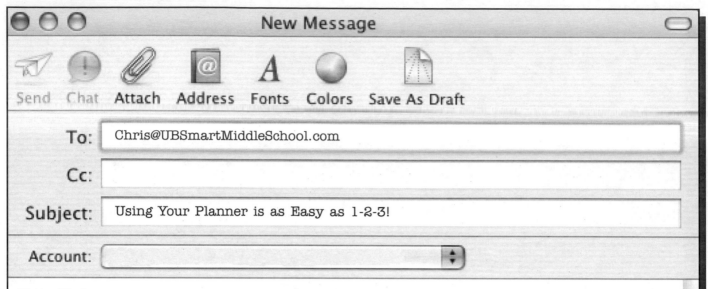

New Message

Send   Chat   **Attach**   **Address**   **Fonts**   **Colors**   **Save As Draft**

To: Chris@UBSmartMiddleSchool.com

Cc:

Subject: Using Your Planner is as Easy as 1-2-3!

Account:

Dear Chris,

Using your planner is as easy as 1-2-3!

1. Your planner should contain important school-wide dates and events, such as exam weeks, bell schedule changes, breaks and holidays. This information is found in your school's **annual calendar** which can be found in the school office or on the school's website.

2. Your planner should contain all important dates and assignments for each of your classes. These are things like homework and project due dates, tests, quizzes and field trips. This information is found in the **class schedule**, which will be provided by each of your teachers at the start of the school year and periodically thereafter. Some teachers provide handouts for students, some post the class schedule on their web page. Copy information from your class schedule into your planner. Carry your planner with you to every class. Listen for any changes or additions to your class schedule. Write the information in your planner!

3. Finally, your planner should contain your **personal schedule**, including doctors and dentist appointments, sports practices, after-school activities, birthdays and vacations. Always note any dates you will be missing school due to personal obligations. Let your teacher know about those dates in advance, so he or she can plan for your absence. Share your schedule with adults that need to know, such as parents, car pool drivers, and coaches.

There you have it! In a nutshell, your planner should contain your (1) school, (2) class and (3) personal schedules.

Sincerely,

Blabby

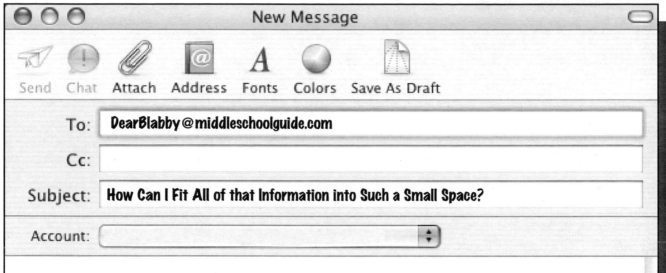

New Message

Send   Chat   Attach   Address   Fonts   Colors   Save As Draft

To: **DearBlabby@middleschoolguide.com**

Cc:

Subject: **How Can I Fit All of that Information into Such a Small Space?**

Account:

Dear Blabby:

Got it! My planner should contain my school, class and personal schedules!

I picked up a copy of my school's annual calendar in the office and copied important dates into my planner. My mom almost fainted when I was able to tell her the exact dates of winter break, but she's okay now. Then I copied important class dates into my planner, including homework assignments and project due dates. I bring my planner with me to every class and write down assignments and schedule changes as soon as I hear them.

I also put important personal dates in my planner, like sports practices, vacations, appointments and birthdays. My math teacher almost hyperventilated when I planned to take a math quiz in advance because of an orthodontist appointment, but she's ok now too.

One more problem, I can't fit all the information into such a small space. Yesterday, I ran out of room, so I wrote an assignment on my hand instead of in my planner. Then I lost all of the information when I showered after P.E. What can I do?

Chris

First Stop: The Middle School Tool Shed

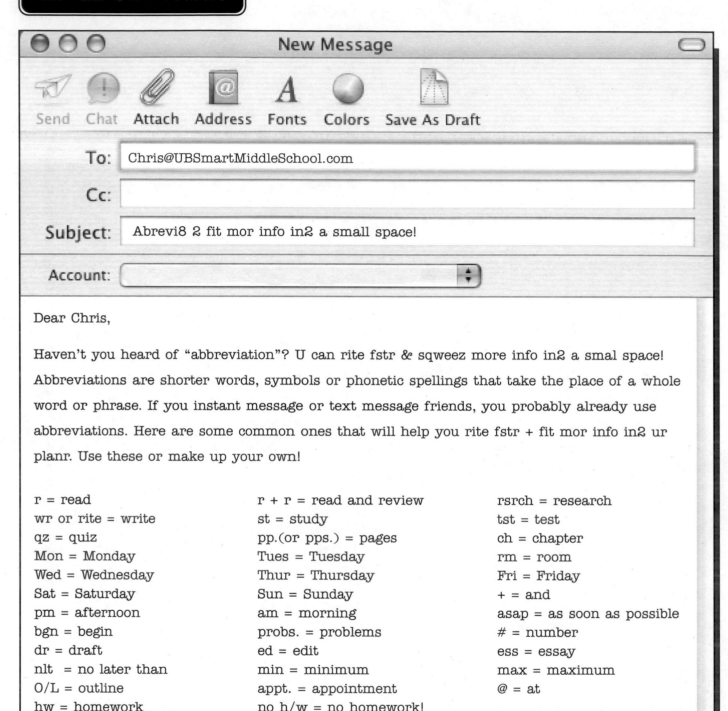

○○○   New Message

Send   Chat   Attach   Address   Fonts   Colors   Save As Draft

To: Chris@UBSmartMiddleSchool.com

Cc:

Subject: Abrevi8 2 fit mor info in2 a small space!

Account:

Dear Chris,

Haven't you heard of "abbreviation"? U can rite fstr & sqweez more info in2 a smal space! Abbreviations are shorter words, symbols or phonetic spellings that take the place of a whole word or phrase. If you instant message or text message friends, you probably already use abbreviations. Here are some common ones that will help you rite fstr + fit mor info in2 ur planr. Use these or make up your own!

r = read	r + r = read and review	rsrch = research
wr or rite = write	st = study	tst = test
qz = quiz	pp.(or pps.) = pages	ch = chapter
Mon = Monday	Tues = Tuesday	rm = room
Wed = Wednesday	Thur = Thursday	Fri = Friday
Sat = Saturday	Sun = Sunday	+ = and
pm = afternoon	am = morning	asap = as soon as possible
bgn = begin	probs. = problems	# = number
dr = draft	ed = edit	ess = essay
nlt = no later than	min = minimum	max = maximum
O/L = outline	appt. = appointment	@ = at
hw = homework	no h/w = no homework!	

Abbreviate names of months as Jan., Feb., Mar., etc., or use the month's numerical representation (i.e., Sept. = 9, Jan. = 1, etc.). Separate planner entries by bullet points (•) to keep information organized.

Sincerely,

Blabby

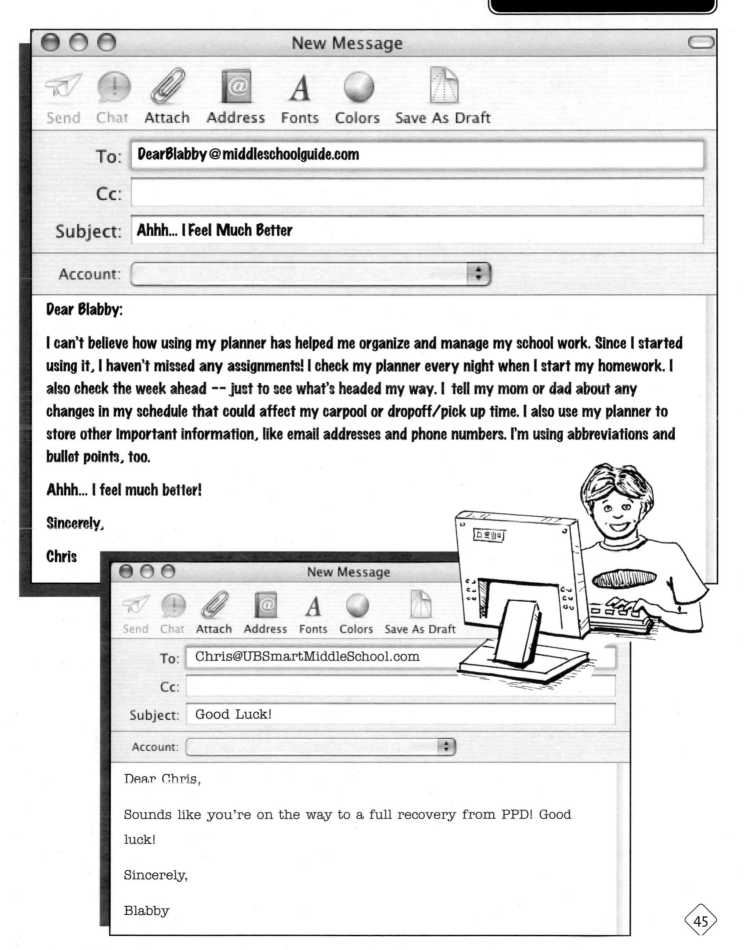

New Message

Send   Chat   Attach   Address   Fonts   Colors   Save As Draft

To: DearBlabby@middleschoolguide.com

Cc:

Subject: Ahhh... I Feel Much Better

Account:

Dear Blabby:

I can't believe how using my planner has helped me organize and manage my school work. Since I started using it, I haven't missed any assignments! I check my planner every night when I start my homework. I also check the week ahead -- just to see what's headed my way. I tell my mom or dad about any changes in my schedule that could affect my carpool or dropoff/pick up time. I also use my planner to store other important information, like email addresses and phone numbers. I'm using abbreviations and bullet points, too.

Ahhh... I feel much better!

Sincerely,

Chris

New Message

Send   Chat   Attach   Address   Fonts   Colors   Save As Draft

To: Chris@UBSmartMiddleSchool.com

Cc:

Subject: Good Luck!

Account:

Dear Chris,

Sounds like you're on the way to a full recovery from PPD! Good luck!

Sincerely,

Blabby

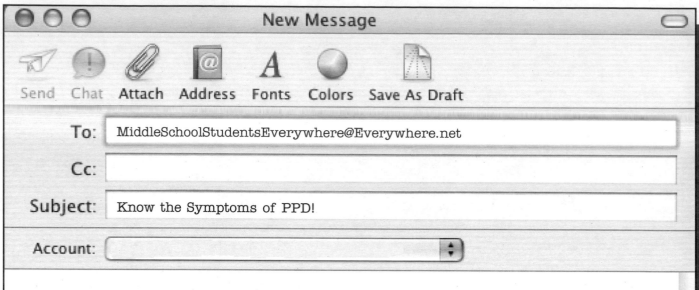

New Message

Send Chat **Attach Address Fonts Colors Save As Draft**

To: MiddleSchoolStudentsEverywhere@Everywhere.net

Cc:

Subject: Know the Symptoms of PPD!

Account:

Dear Middle School Students:

Tragically, Personal Planner Disorder ("PPD") can strike any middle school student at any time. If treated, it is 100% curable. I urge each of you to learn to recognize the symptoms of PPD. They are:

✛ Late or missing assignments;

✛ Butterflies in the stomach when thinking about school or homework;

✛ Finishing assignments or studying for tests at the last minute, often late into the night;

✛ Forgetting class or bell schedule changes;

✛ Forgetting homework changes;

✛ Funny looks from teachers or parents; (Well, that could be a symptom of almost anything);

✛ Parents who are annoyed with your report card;

If you think you may have PPD, don't take chances. Reach for your planner and start using it immediately! Good luck!

Sincerely,

Blabby

The Middle School Student's Guide to Ruling the World!

Let's Practice Middle School Work Management and Organizational Skills!

The Planner

Hooray, it's Friday! It's been a busy week at middle school. You expect next week to be even busier. This morning, your math teacher assigned a quiz for Monday. It will cover chapters 4 and 5. You'll need to study this weekend! Your history teacher assigned pages 223–240 of the textbook to be read and outlined by Wednesday's class. Your science report and vocabulary cards are due on Thursday. The deadline to hand in the permission slip for the field trip to the zoo is 3:00 on Tuesday (in Room 131). You have band practice from 3:00–5:00 on Tuesday. There's a basketball game on Friday at 3:30. Saturday is your dad's birthday. Don't forget your orthodontist appointment on Friday at 11:00!

Below is a blank page from a typical middle school weekly planner. Schedule your responsibilities for the next week in the correct spaces. Use abbreviations and bullet points!

Today

Monday	Tuesday	Wednesday	Thursday	Friday	Sat/Sun
Monday	Tuesday	Wednesday	Thursday	Friday	Sat/Sun

How did you do? Check your answers on page 169.

Notes:

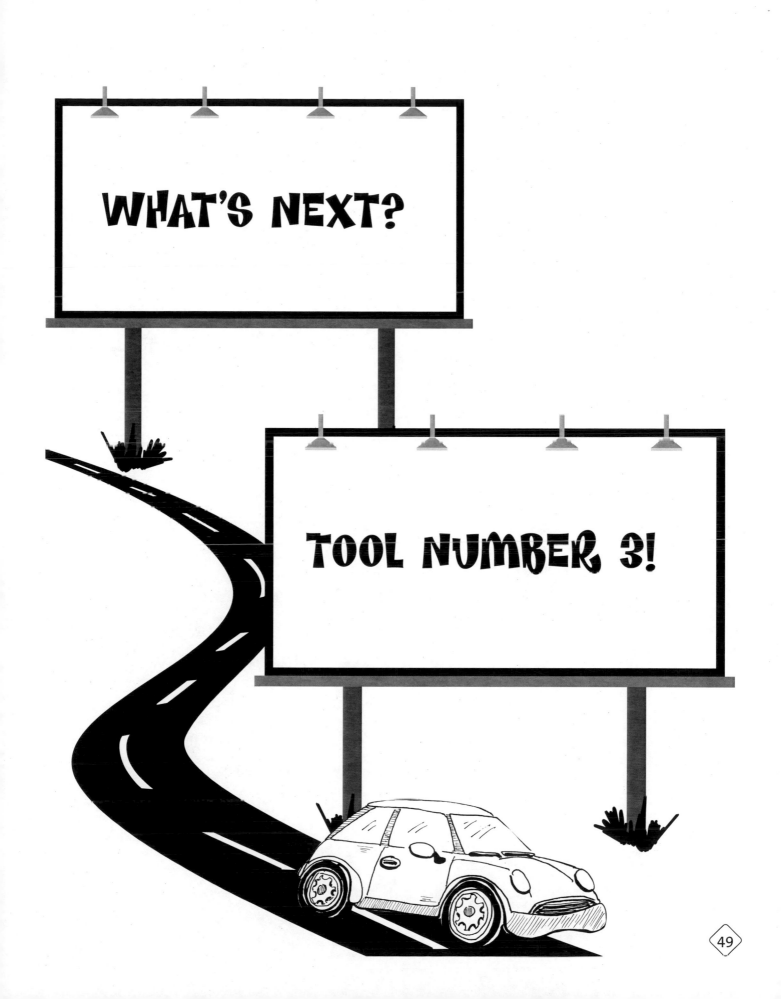

Tool Number 3:
The Study Bud

What is a study bud? A study bud is a classmate you know and can rely on for support, back up and information sharing. A study bud helps his or her study bud partner in the event of confusion about a homework assignment or project, or if the study bud is out sick for a couple of days, and needs to know what happened in class. It is a two way relationship – students helping one another. Study buds can also share books, study together, pair up on projects or fax missing assignment pages. A reliable study bud is an important tool for success in middle school.

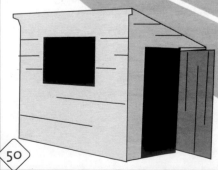

AWESOME STUDY BUDS FOR LARRY

Okay, a study bud isn't *really* a superhero! But a good study bud can occasionally rescue you from the brink of disaster. After my latest homework emergency, I lined up a study bud for each of my classes. Now I have a classmate I can contact if I forget to write down an assignment, forget a book at school, or if I've lost a worksheet or handout. Like, last week when I was out sick for three days, my study bud picked up handouts for me and called to give me a heads up on a change in a reading assignment. It was a big help. (Thanks, dude.)

Hey! Before you start thinking that having a study bud gives you a license to slack, check out these rules:

STUDY BUD RULES

✔ Study bud time is business only. When you call, I.M. or text message a study bud, don't waste time gossiping or socializing. Be respectful of your study bud's time.

✔ Observe your study bud's phone call cut off time. Don't call too late; don't call too early.

✔ Before contacting your study bud, try to solve the problem yourself. Check your notes, handouts and the class website. If you still can't figure it out, go ahead and contact your study bud.

✔ Give your study bud reliable information. If you don't know or you're not sure, say so!

✔ Don't expect a free ride on your study bud and don't allow your study bud a free ride on you.

✔ A study bud should never be anyone your crush'n!

STUDY BUDS RULE!

It's awesome to have a study bud in a homework emergency. Ask one classmate in each of your classes to be your study bud. Exchange information on this Study Bud 4-1-1 form. Keep it in a sheet protector in your binder. Here's a blank Study Bud 4-1-1 that you can copy and use for getting the 4-1-1 on your Study Bud. You can also go to www.middleschoolguide.com to download and print as many as you need!

STUDY BUD 4-1-1

Class: _____

Study Bud: _____

Address: _____

Email address: _____

Home Phone: _____

IM: _____

Cell Phone: _____

Fax No: _____

Phone call cut off time: _____

STUDYING WITH STUDY BUDS

Once in a while, you might get together with your study bud or a group of classmates to study or review for a test or quiz. In high school, students often study in groups, so learning how to study with a group now is good practice for the future.

Studying with another person, or a group of students can be helpful because you can exchange ideas, compare notes and share the load. But it can be a waste of time, if the group doesn't work well together, or if the study session becomes too social. Here are some things you can do to get the most out of studying with your buds:

1

Know what to study. You won't believe how many students study the wrong materials before an exam! If your group is studying for an exam or quiz, start the study session by reviewing together the teacher's instructions about the test. What information or chapters will be covered? Will the test be multiple choice or essay? Will certain areas be given more weight than others for grading? Are any special materials required for the test?

The Middle School Student's Guide to Ruling the World!

2

Use your time wisely. Check notes, chapter headings and study guides to get an idea of how many items your group needs to review in the time you've set aside for the study session. Study groups often spend too much time on the first few items, then run out of time before they get to the rest. If you have twenty items to review, and have set aside two hours for the study session, you have only 6 minutes per item (120 minutes ÷ by 20 items = 6 minutes per item). That's <u>without</u> factoring in a break! Ask a member of the group to keep track of the time and to speak up when the group is spending too much time on one topic or is getting off task.

3

Share the load. At the start of the study session or a day or two before if you have the chance, divide the study topics among the study buds. Each student is responsible to "teach" or lead the discussion on one or more items. That way, each study bud contributes equally.

4

Keep breaks short. No more than 10 minutes per hour of studying. Save the chill'n and snack'n for after the study session!

HOW TO SUCCESSFULLY MANAGE
GROUP PROJECTS
OR
HOW TO TAKE THE "GRRRRR" OUT OF GROUPS

"Last semester, my science teacher assigned a group project. I was put in a group with three other kids in my class. It turned out to be one of the most frustrating experiences of my middle school life. We argued a lot over how to get the work done. Some of the group members felt that they had worked harder and contributed more to the project than others. Some kids forgot to go to the group meetings and one kid (uh, that would be me) was late getting his part of the project done. Not cool."

"A few weeks ago, my history teacher assigned a group project. The project was to make a dramatic presentation of the Boston Tea Party using a poster, props and a script. I totally dreaded another group project. Then I realized that, just like studying with buds, there are ways to make a group project run smoothly."

good communication

sharing the load

defining tasks

sharing ideas

setting group goals

careful planning

Larry's Awesome Group Project Organizer

Good communication and careful planning are important for a successful group project. So, as soon as the project was assigned, I designed a "Group Project Organizer." It's a form we used to exchange contact information, share ideas, create a project plan and schedule productive group meetings.

I brought a blank Group Project Organizer to our first group meeting. At the meeting, we passed it around and each member filled in their own name, phone numbers and email information.

Then our group reviewed the project instructions. As we made decisions about how to complete the project, I filled in the organizer with the correct information. I made sure that each group member got a copy of the Group Project Organizer the very next day. It really helped our group successfully manage our project. Check out my masterpiece on the next page. ➜ ➜ ➜ ➜ ➜ ➜ ➜ ➜

LARRY'S (AWESOME) GROUP PROJECT ORGANIZER

2

Class: American History (4th Period)   **Project:** Boston Tea Party Presentation   **Group Leader:** Larry

Name	Phone #	Cell Phone #	Email Address
Larry **1**	555-1278	555-6335	larry@UBSmartMiddleSchool.com
Angela	555-2625	no cell	angela@youemailme2.com
Chan	555-5151	no cell	chantheman@chantheman.net
Ana	555-4622	555-8725	ana@youemailme3.com

Project Tasks (Describe Fully)		Assigned To
1. Write a 6 page script. Make copies for everyone in the group by Friday 11/6. Play **3** part of Samuel Adams. Memorize by Thurs. Email biography to Angela by Friday.		Larry
2. Create a poster of the highlights of the Boston Tea Party by 11/12. Play the part of a colonist. Email the biography of character to Angela by Friday. Memorize lines.		Chan
3. Make the play program. Add biographical info. Do cover artwork. Email my characters' biography to Angela by 11/15. Play a Native American. Write biography of Paul Revere.		Ana
4. Write proclamation about Townsend Acts. Put it on parchment in colonial writing. Email clip art for program to Ana. Play the part of Native American. Send biography to Angela by 11/15.		Angela

Project Supplies	Due Date	Assigned To
· Costumes: (Colonial and Native American) **4**	By Thurs. 11/12 meeting	Ana & Larry
· A lantern (Colonial style)	By last group meeting	Chan
· 3 cartons painted like barrels, and filled with pieces of brown paper to look like tea.	By last group meeting	Angela

Group Meeting Date	Time	Place	Goals
Mon (11/9)	3:30 to 4:30	School Library	Read the script together. Practice parts.
Thurs (11/12) **5**	3:30 to 4:30	School Library	Review poster. Rehearse play in costume. **6**
Tues (11/17)	3:30 to 4:30	School Library	Rehearse play with lines memorized.
Weds. (11/18)	7:00 - 8:30	Chan's house 108 Maple Dr.	Final rehearsal with props, costumes and poster. Review and correct program biographies.

1

Communication Information

Group members exchanged phone numbers and email addresses. That made communication a lot easier!

2

Group Leader

I volunteered to be our group leader. It's the group leader's job to fill out the Group Project Organizer and make sure that everyone gets a copy. The group leader also keeps the group on task at project meetings.

Defining Tasks

We reviewed our teacher's instructions for the project. Everyone had a chance to express their ideas about how to do the project. (There are lots of good ideas out there!) After we agreed on how to do the project, then we split the work into "tasks." Tasks were divided as evenly as possible so that nobody felt that they had a lot more work to do than anyone else. Each task was carefully described, so when the meeting was over, we each knew *exactly* what our job was, where and when our part of the project was due.

3

Goals for Meetings

It's important to have a goal for each group meeting. That way, we knew exactly what we had to accomplish, so we didn't goof around.

Supplies

Supplies are important! Our group decided what kind of supplies or props were needed, and who would be responsible for getting them.

4

5

Group Meetings

This is our group meeting schedule. To minimize confusion, we tried to schedule group meetings at the same place and time.

6

Check out page 60 for a Group Project Organizer you can copy and use for your next group project.

First Stop: The Middle School Tool Shed

GROUP PROJECT ORGANIZER

Class: _____ Project: _____ Group Leader: _____

Name	Phone #	Cell Phone #	Email Address

Project Tasks (Describe Fully)	Assigned To

Project Supplies	Due Date	Assigned To

Group Meeting Date	Time	Place	Goals

The Middle School Student's Guide to Ruling the World!

Let's Practice Middle School Work Management and Organizational Skills!

The Study Bud

1. When you're on study bud time, it's _____ only!

    a. business   b. games   c. gossip   d. fun

2. Always respect your study bud's _____.

    a. right to party   b. phone call cut-off time
    c. hairstyle   d. all of the above

3. Do your best to give your study bud _____ information.

    a. false   b. top secret   c. reliable   d. useless

4. When you study with a bud or a group of buds:

    a. Know what you need to study.
    b. Keep breaks short.
    c. Share the load!
    d. All of the above

5. You're studying for a social studies test with a group of study buds. You've set aside an hour and a half (90 minutes) for the study session. You review chapter headings and your teacher's instructions about the test. There are ten items to be studied. At some point, your group wants to take a 10 minute break. You have about _____ minutes to study each item.

6. Exchanging _____ makes communication easier among project group members.

    a. home phone numbers
    b. email addresses
    c. cell phone numbers
    d. all of the above

7. Why is it important to have a goal for each group project meeting?

    _____

    _____

    _____

8. A study bud can be a big help when:

    a. you are absent from school and need someone to pick up handouts for you.
    b. you forget to write down an assignment.
    c. you left your workbook at school and need a copy of the page assigned for homework.
    d. all of the above

9. You have been picked to be the Group Leader for your group project. It is *your* responsibility to:

    a. complete the Group Project Organizer at the first project meeting.
    b. make sure that each group member gets a copy of the completed Group Project Organizer.
    c. keep your group on task at project meetings.
    d. all of the above

10. Your science teacher has just assigned a group project. You are bummed because on the last group project, you ended up doing most of the work. How can this problem be avoided on the new project?

    a. Beg your teacher to reassign you to a group of overachievers.
    b. Ask for independent study instead.
    c. Go to www.middleschoolguide.com to download a copy of the Group Project Organizer. Bring it to the first group meeting and use it to successfully organize your group project!
    d. Do a good job on your part of the project and hope for the best.

How did you do? Check your answers on page 169.

Notes:

Tool Number 4: The Teacher

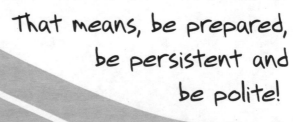

Please take a number and get in line.

As one of the most powerful tools in the Middle School Tool Shed, your teacher is an important resource to help you manage your workload. But, did you know that a typical middle school teacher teaches about 100 students per day? Most teachers are patient and are happy to be of assistance whenever students need help. Others may be abrupt or short – not because they're mean or don't like students, but because they have so many that need their attention! Help your teacher to help you by being a responsible middle school student. That means, be prepared, be persistent and be polite!

HOW TO IMPRESS A MIDDLE SCHOOL TEACHER

Sometimes Jamal feels like a small fish in a very big middle school pond. He's shy and quiet, and he's uncertain of what his teachers expect of him, now that he's in middle school. He's heard teachers tell the students to "be responsible." Curious about what this means to teachers, Jamal has been doing some research...

**IMPRESS
SCHOOL TEACHER**

**HOW TO IMPRESS
A MIDDLE SCHOOL TEACHER**

Introduction:
What Do Middle School Teachers Want?

Middle school teachers come in every shape and size, and from all walks of life, but they all have one thing in common: They want their students to be *responsible*. What does this mean to a teacher? It means that they want students to be prepared, be persistent and be polite!

Chapter 1:
Be Prepared!

Try to Solve the Problem Yourself.

Most middle school teachers are happy to help you with a problem and are grateful when you come to them for assistance rather than let the matter (and your grade) slide. But, if you've lost a worksheet, or are unsure of a test date or have any other

work management problem, try to tackle it yourself before going to your teacher. Check your class schedule, handouts, notes and website. Call your study bud. If you've done your best, but still can't solve the problem, ask away! Let your teacher know that you have tried to solve the problem yourself. Your efforts to be a responsible student will impress your teacher.

Practice Saying It!

Are you uncomfortable talking to your teacher or asking for help? Are you too shy or do you sometimes get tongue-tied or feel rushed? If so, practice what you are going to say before talking to him or her. You don't have to memorize a full speech. Practice your question by saying it aloud. It will help you explain your problem more clearly. That will help you feel more comfortable and confident when you talk to your teacher.

**HOW TO IMPRESS
A MIDDLE SCHOOL TEACHER**

Chapter 2:
Be Persistent!

Follow Up on Matters that Affect Your Grade.

Your middle school teacher has an interest in making sure that the grade you receive is accurate. But, with so many students to keep track of, they occasionally make mistakes in grading. Some errors are obvious, such as an error in addition. (Always check your teacher's addition on a grade sheet.) If you've received an incorrect score on a test or essay, politely bring it to the attention of your teacher so it can be corrected.

What if you think that a teacher has given you an unfair grade on a test, project or essay? It is perfectly acceptable to discuss the score with your teacher and explain why you think it should be higher. But, before you do, make sure you can state precisely why you believe you deserve a change of grade. Be specific—"it's not fair" doesn't go over. Being persistent is good. Being argumentative is bad. Remember, your teacher has the final word!

**HOW TO IMPRESS
A MIDDLE SCHOOL TEACHER**

It's Your Responsibility to Get What You Need.

Middle school teachers are busy with lots of students needing their attention. Sometimes they lose track of things or forget obligations. Everybody does. If your teacher has promised to help you with a matter, such as getting you another copy of a handout or changing a grade for you, it is *your* responsibility to follow up! If your teacher has forgotten, politely remind him or her of what you need. If you were absent from class for any reason, it is *your* responsibility to follow up with your teacher to find out what you missed.

Report Problems Understanding the Subject.

What if you've been listening in class, studying hard, keeping up with homework, but are still having problems understanding the subject? Let your teacher know. Don't be shy! Your teacher wants you to succeed. He or she will be able to help you, or point you in the direction of other resources, such as a tutoring program, homework club or helpful website.

Chapter 3: Be Polite!

Listen in Class.

Middle school teachers work hard to help you develop the skills and knowledge you'll need to make a smooth transition to high school. It's no easy job. They deserve your respect. The best way to show respect for your teacher is to listen in class. Sit up, keep your eyes on the teacher when he or she is talking and look interested. Answer politely when your teacher talks to you. Don't joke around or encourage others to be silly or rude.

Get Involved!

It's not easy for a teacher to stand up in front of a class day after day trying to generate interest in a subject. Help your teacher out by participating in class. Your participation will encourage other students to get involved. You might also find that you're good at a subject or (gasp!) that you actually like it. Participating in class is one of the best ways your teacher can get to know you. If you're shy or unsure of yourself, start your answer by saying, "Well, I'm not sure, but…" Once you do it a few times, you'll gain confidence in your ability to speak up. It's a skill you'll need for high school, so start practicing now!

Say Thanks!

Thank your teacher whenever he or she takes time to help you. If your teacher has spent a large amount of time helping you, or has given up a break or stayed after school to help you, write a short thank you note (binder paper is okay). Leave it in their in-box. It will show that you truly appreciated the help. Feel free to compliment your teacher every now and then on something you enjoyed about the class, or something the teacher said or did that made the material fun or easier to understand. Everybody likes to hear that they have done a good job—even teachers!

Take Responsibility for Your Mistakes.

Being polite also means taking responsibility for your actions whenever you've made a mistake, misbehaved, broken a rule, or are in hot water with your teacher for any reason. Don't waste your teacher's time or test his or her patience by making excuses or blaming someone else. Apologize, face the consequences and move on! That may not get you out of trouble, but your honesty and maturity will impress your teacher.

HOW TO
IMPRESS
A
MIDDLE

Let's Practice Middle School Work Management and Organizational Skills!

The Teacher

Select a word or words from the list below to correctly complete the sentence.

1. Being a responsible student means being _____, _____ and _____!

2. Before asking your middle school teacher for help, try to solve the problem _____.

3. If you discover your teacher has made an error on your grade, bring the matter to his or her attention in a _____ manner.

4. With regard to dealing with teachers, being _____ is good; being _____ is bad!

5. In any disagreement about a grade, your teacher has the _____ word!

6. "Being persistent" means _____ on matters that affect your grade!

7. If you are uncomfortable talking to a teacher, first _____ what you are going to say.

8. State four ways to be polite to your teacher: (1) _____ (2) _____ (3) _____ (4) _____.

9. Always _____ your teacher's addition on a grading sheet.

10. Let your teacher know if you are having problems. Your teacher wants you to _____!

polite	following up	listen in class	succeed
persistant; argumentative	prepared; persistent; polite	participate in class	final
yourself	practice	say thank you	apologize
		recheck	

How did you do? Check your answers on page 169.

Notes:

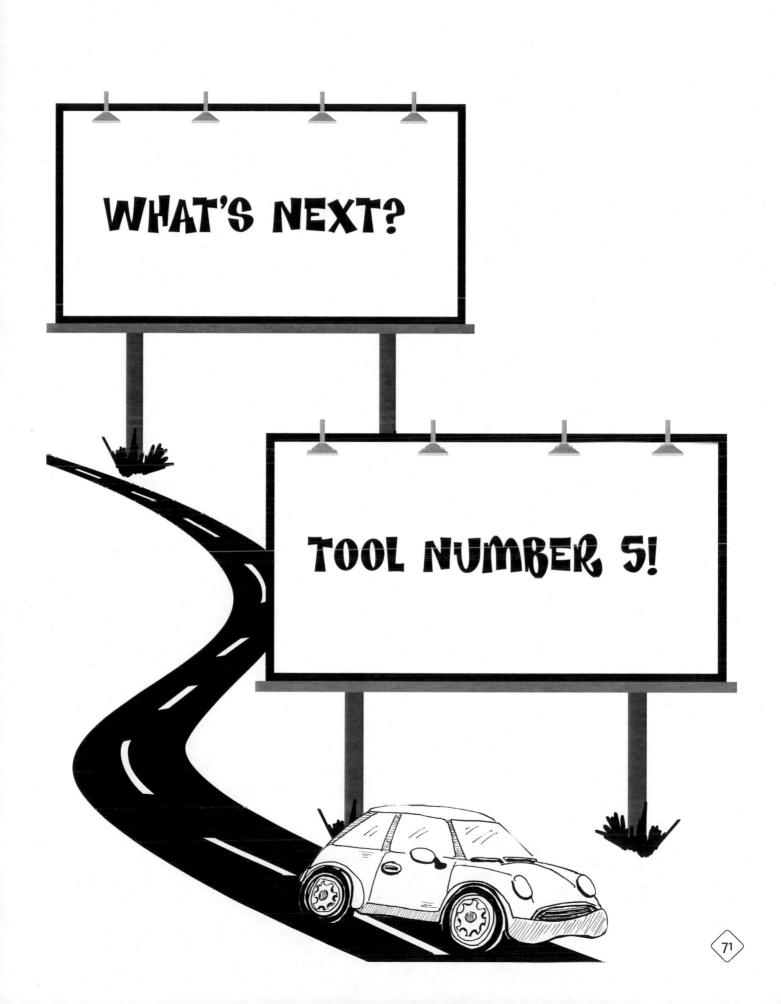

Tool Number 5:
Class Notes

Taking notes in class is an excellent way to improve your middle school work management and organizational skills. As you take notes, you concentrate on, and process more of what your teacher is saying. You're less likely to be distracted by friends and less prone to daydreaming. Taking notes reinforces what you are learning, and can actually reduce the amount of time you'll need to study for a test. Even better, class notes create a kind of journal of the things your teacher wants you to know and to do! So, when you're in class, go ahead, tune in and take "to know" and "to do" notes!

POLLY'S MOM, MOLLY, IS CHECKING OUT HOW POLLY'S BEEN DOING ON HER WEEKLY BIOLOGY QUIZZES AND SHE'S NOT TOO HAPPY WITH HER SCORES.

POLLY, ACCORDING TO THESE SCORES, IT'S PRETTY OBVIOUS THAT YOU NEED TO PAY MORE ATTENTION IN CLASS!

I TRY MOM, BUT IT'S HARD TO REMEMBER ALL THAT COMPLICATED STUFF MY TEACHER SAYS AND SOMETIMES I GET SLEEPY OR MY FRIENDS DISTRACT ME FROM WHAT'S GOING ON IN CLASS.

POLLY, HAVEN'T YOU EVER HEARD OF TAKING NOTES?

HUH?

TAKING NOTES WILL HELP YOU CONCENTRATE ON WHAT YOUR TEACHER IS SAYING AND KEEP YOU FROM BEING DISTRACTED BY FRIENDS. ALSO, NOTES ARE A REALLY BIG HELP WHEN YOU HAVE TO STUDY FOR A TEST OR QUIZ.

POLLY, HAVEN'T YOU EVER TAKEN NOTES IN CLASS?

NO MOM, I'VE NEVER ACTUALLY TAKEN NOTES, BUT I'VE SURE PASSED A LOT OF THEM!

TUN'N IN & TAK'N NOTES
WITH POLLY (AND MOLLY)

"True story. Sometimes I had a hard time paying attention in class. I was distracted, or not that interested in what my teacher was saying. I missed out on directions about assignments and homework. I daydreamed and looked forward to class being over so I could get back to talking with my friends. After seeing the scores on my last progress report, my mom Molly, made it clear that I'd better start paying more attention in class!

"Hmmm...I wondered, what could I do? Then I visited the Middle School Tool Shed, and I learned that I could tune in and take notes!

This is me, distracted in class by my friend Sara.

This is me tun'n in and tak'n notes in History.

"Ok, here's the deal... taking notes doesn't mean just pulling out a blank piece of paper and scribbling down everything your teacher says. Good note-taking skills begin with good *listening* skills! Now, the second I pass through the door of my classroom, I have a pen or a pencil in my hand. I stop chatting with friends—that was the hard part for me. I go to my desk. I open my planner to the correct date. I open my binder to a clean piece of binder paper. I write the date at the top. Then, I tune in and *listen* for two different, but equally important kinds of information: What my teacher wants me '**TO DO**' and what my teacher wants me '**TO KNOW**.'"

"TO DO" vs. "TO KNOW" information

TO DO information refers to your teacher's directions about homework assignments, projects, class activities, schedules - stuff like that. It's information about what your teacher wants you to do and how your teacher wants you to do it. In middle school it's important that you do things just the way your teacher tells you.

TO KNOW information refers to the stuff your teacher wants you to learn about the subject you are studying.

Taking To DO Notes

1. Homework:

Most of your homework assignments will be on a handout or posted to the class website. But sometimes teachers make adjustments or additions to homework. They change assigned pages or problems, or change due dates. Listen for changes and note them in your planner.

2. Tests and Quizzes:

Always listen for instructions about tests and quizzes. Note special test supplies, like graph paper, red pen, number 2 pencil, calculator, etc. Listen and note the type of test: Will it be essay? Short answer? Multiple choice? Knowing what kind of test you'll be taking helps you know how to study.

3. Lab Books and Journals:

In some middle school classes you'll be required to keep a lab book or a journal. Your teacher will tell you how to set it up. Write the instructions in your notes and follow them carefully. In terms of grading, how well you follow directions for setting up and maintaining a lab book or journal can be just as important what you write in it!

4. Info on Turning Stuff in:

Middle school teachers can be kind of particular about how, when or where they want you to turn in an assignment or project. Consider their turn-in directions to be an important part of the assignment. Listen for instructions, write them in your binder or planner and follow them carefully. Some middle school teachers use web-based turn-in services for papers, essays, and reports. Note login and password instructions in your planner.

5. Projects:

When your teacher assigns a project, he or she will discuss the project requirements, due dates and special supplies. These instructions are important. Listen and write the information in your binder notes. How well you follow project instructions will affect your overall project grade.

6. Permission Slips:

Lots of school activities require signed permission slips. Always note a permission slip deadline in your planner. Make sure it's signed and returned to school on time. If your class is planning a field trip, note the permission slip return deadline, as well as the date of the field trip. Make note of other field trip requirements, such as special costs, supplies, and meals.

Taking To KNOW Notes

Lectures:

- As soon as your teacher begins instruction, listen for the topic of the day. Clues to the topic of the day are words like "today we will be reviewing..." or "today we'll be learning about..." Write the topic at the top of your paper.

- Listen for your teacher to identify the main ideas about the topic and make a note of the main ideas.

- Listen for information that supports the main ideas. Write it down, using abbreviations and bullet points or numbers.

- If your teacher emphasizes important points by writing them on the board, copy the information into your notes. Underline points that have been stressed or repeated by your teacher. They are likely to be covered on a test or quiz.

- If your teacher uses an example to make a point or explain a concept, write down the basic idea of the example. It will help you recall what was taught.

- At the end of class, your teacher may summarize important points that were taught that day. Listen carefully and make sure you've noted all of them.

Did You Miss Something?

If you missed something your teacher said, or you're not sure if you wrote it down correctly, write a question mark next to that section of notes. Before you leave the classroom, ask your teacher to clarify the point.

Math

Have you ever been working on math homework and thought, "Hey! What's going on? In class, I understood how to solve this problem, but now I can't remember how to do it!" Guess what? Notes are for math too! Copy sample problems your teacher uses in class to explain a math concept or formula. Write down what he or she says about solving the problem. These notes are a big help when you have a similar problem for homework.

$$2x - 7 = 3 + x$$

TiP: WHAT'S UP WITH BORING NOTE FORMS?

There's no law that requires middle school students to use plain old binder paper to take notes! Blank binder paper hardly inspires anyone to take meaningful notes. Try designing your own class note forms on your computer's word processing program. Mix it up! You can decorate your note forms with photos, artwork or clip art. Customize your note forms to guide you to take good notes. Print 20–25 copies of your masterpiece and place them in the binder paper section of your binder. Check out these websites for some PDF note forms and graphic organizers that can help you tune in and take awesome class notes:

- Houghton Mifflin Education Place
  www.eduplace.com

- Tools for Reading Writing + Thinking
  www.greece.k12.ny.us

- S.C.O.R.E Graphic Organizers
  www.sdcoe.k12.ca.us/score/actbank/torganiz.htm

Welcome to your 5th period American history class. You've walked into the classroom, you've stopped talking with friends and you're seated at your desk. You have your pencil in hand, and your planner and binder open. Great! You're tun'n and tak'n notes! Here's what your history teacher has to say today. Your job: circle the "to do" information and underline the "to know" information. Then answer the questions below.

"Good afternoon class. Will everyone please settle down? We have a lot to do today. Just a reminder, the Chapter 5 test is this Friday. It will consist of twenty multiple choice questions and five short answers. Bring two no. 2 sharpened pencils to class that day, as well as your 1812 Map handout. Okay class, today we're continuing with the topic of the War of 1812. Oh, one more reminder, please return all library books by Wednesday! If your book is not returned by Wednesday, I will take 2 points off of your test score. Also, please make sure that, no later than next Wednesday, you have selected the subject for your biographical report. Submit the name of the historical character to me on a lined 3x5 index card. The card must include the name and the birth date of the character and a reason why you have selected that person. One of you asked me whether Homer Simpson may be considered an important American historical figure. The answer is no. Now, continuing with our lesson. Today there are two things I want you to understand about the War of 1812. First, it is the war that made America a power on the international stage. Secondly, the War of 1812 opened the old Northwest to settlement..."

1. What is the "topic" of the day? _____

2. What are the two main ideas? _____ and _____

3. What information must be included on the biography index card? _____

_____

4. What two things must you do by Wednesday? _____ and _____

5. What will happen if your library book is not returned by Wednesday? _____

_____

How did you do? Check your answers on page 170.

Notes:

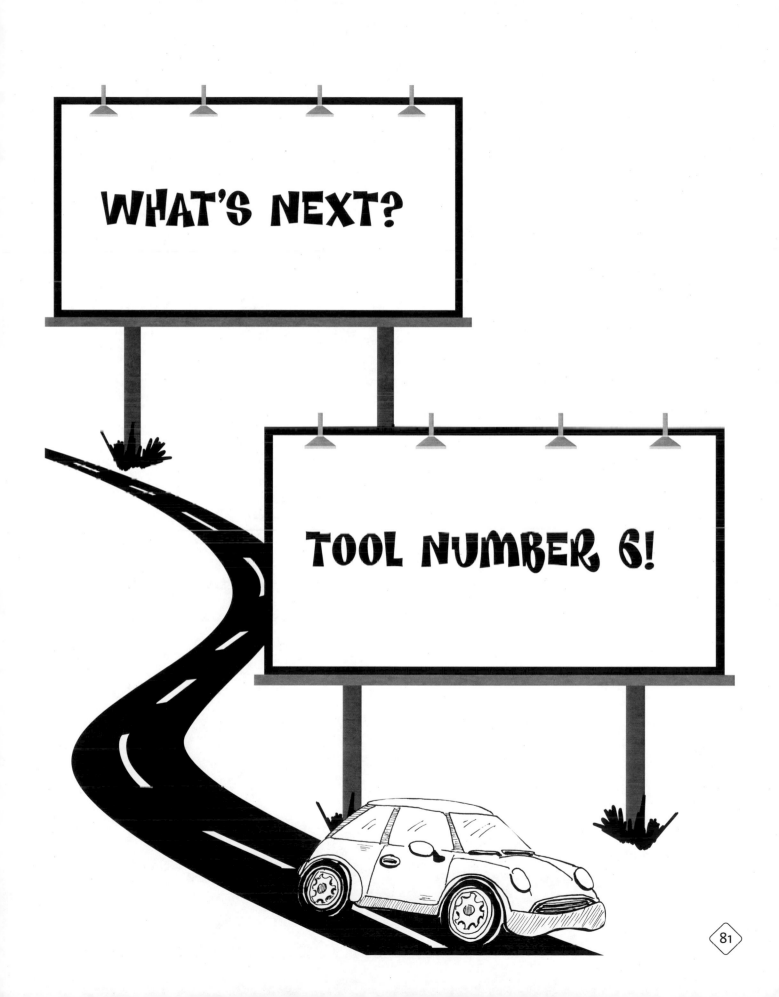

Tool Number 6:
Your Workspace

In the business world, it is a well-known fact that a worker's productivity increases (or decreases) depending upon their surroundings. People are happier and work more efficiently when they have a space of their own to work in, which is organized and stocked with the supplies they need to get the job done. It is no different for middle school students. The space where you study and do homework affects the quality of your work and your ability to manage your time. In short, an organized and well-stocked workspace is an important tool for success in middle school.

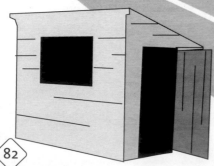

HOW TO ORGANIZE A WORKSPACE THAT ROCKS!

By Late Larry

OK. I confess! I was a homework nomad. I wandered from place to place to do homework...

One night I'd be at the dining room table...

The next night I'd work at the kitchen counter...

Some nights, I'd "work" on the couch...

Sometimes I'd do my homework in my room, where my so-called "workspace" looked like a disaster area. I never had the supplies I needed. I never used a dictionary or a thesaurus 'cause I could never find them. I spent so much time just getting *ready* to do my homework, I hardly ever had enough time to finish it!

At the Middle School Tool Shed, I learned that my nomadic homework routine and my messy workspace were making me work harder and longer than I needed to. Not cool. I learned that the space where I work affects the quality of my work and my ability to manage my time.

So, I got going! I found a quiet, private place that is well lit and free from stuff that distracts me. I stocked it with the supplies I need for homework. Now I'm doing my *best* work in the *least* amount of time. That means I have more time to do stuff I really like to do! Cool. My workspace rocks.

OK, so here's a heads up:
A good workspace is more than just a desk and a couple of pencils. I made a checklist to help you set up a workspace that rocks! First find a quiet place for your workspace—some place that's free from distractions. Then use this checklist to help you deck it out with all of the supplies you need to do your *best* work in the *least* amount of time!

Let's Practice Middle School Work Management and Organizational Skills!

Your Organized Workspace

Ok, it's time to get your workspace organized! Use this form to take an inventory. What have you got? What do you need? Make a plan to get what you need. (You can also go to www.middleschoolguide.com to download and print this form!)

Item	What it is!	Got it!	Need it!	My plan to get it:
• Location	Quiet and comfortable; Away from distractions like t.V., stereo, phones, video games and people talking. This could be your bedroom or anywhere else in your house.			
• Computer	Access to a computer with a printer is important for middle school, but if the computer is a distraction for you, don't keep it at your workspace!			
• Desk or table	A desktop surface should be at least 18" deep and 30" wide – large enough to hold an open textbook and binder.			
• Lighting	Good lighting is important! A desktop lamp will help prevent eye strain that can make you feel tired and sleepy.			
• Chair	Straight-backed and comfortable.			
• Reference Books	A dictionary, a thesaurus and a grammar & punctuation guide. If you are taking a foreign language course, you'll need a dictionary in that language, too.			
• Supplies	Binder paper, #2 pencils, pens, markers, colored pencils, a ruler (metric and standard measurements), glue stick, yellow highlighter, scissors, scotch tape, a stapler and staples, three hole punch, index cards (blank and lined), an eraser, white out, paper clips and a pencil sharpener. Don't forget your math supplies!			
• Trash can	Keep your desk top clean and clutter free!			
• Storage	Use a box, accordion file or several large manila envelopes to store graded papers, class notes, and handouts you may need later.			
• Time Keeper	A clock or a watch.			
• In-box	A low-profile basket or box to keep papers from piling up your desk.			
• Fun stuff!	Photos of your buds, team photos, cool posters, stickers, decals, notes, etc. Make your workspace a place where you won't mind hanging out!			

DO YOU HAVE TWO HOMES?

Kids whose parents are divorced sometimes split their time between two homes. If you go between homes, you may need to set up two workspaces. There's no need to double up on supplies. That can be costly. Keep your supplies in a backpack or easy-to-tote box and take them with you when you go!

DO YOU SHARE A ROOM?

If you share a room with a brother or sister who won't go away when you need some quiet time to do your homework, don't argue or fight about it. Ask your mom or dad to set and enforce a time every day when you can have the room all to yourself to do homework. Stick to the schedule!

Notes:

Tool Number 7:
The Rubric

Ms. Lophat's Rubric for Healthy Meal Poster Project

CRITERIA	SCORE			
The Healthy Meal Poster includes a graphic or photos of a balanced and healthy meal.	4	3	2	1
Each of the graphics or photos of the balanced and healthy meal are labeled to identify 1) the food pictured **and** 2) the food group to which the food belongs.	4	3	2	1
The student attaches typewritten lab notes which include:				
• A statement of the reasons for the foods selected.	4	3	2	1
• A description of three safety procedures he/she would use if when preparing the meal.	4	3	2	1
The poster includes two 3x5 unlined index cards indentifying (1) the name of a book on nutrition for teens, including the title, author and number of pages; and (2) a recipe for one of the items served in the "balanced meal".	4	3	2	1
Appearance of the student's poster:				
• Poster is neat and legible.				
• Uses correct grammar and spelling	4	3	2	1
• Contains student's name, date and class period in lower right corner.	4	3	2	1
	4	3	2	1

Middle school teachers often provide students with written directions how to succeed in their class. These directions are called "rubrics." When you receive a rubric, pay close attention! It will tell you exactly what you need to do to get a good grade on a project, paper or assignment. It's like having the answers right in front of you and it's totally legal! So, when your teacher is kind enough to provide you with a rubric, be smart enough to use it.

First Stop: The Middle School Tool Shed

JAMAL LEARNS
THE RULES OF RUBRIC ROAD

Student Survey

Check "yes" or "no." Have you ever:

	YES	NO
1. installed a computer game?	☐	☐
2. downloaded music?	☐	☐
3. made a batch of cookies (or otherwise followed a recipe)?	☐	☐
4. helped your mom or dad read a road map on a trip?	☐	☐
5. followed the rules to a board game?	☐	☐

IF YOU ANSWERED "YES" to any of these survey questions, you've proven that you *can* understand and follow directions! Installation guides, rule sheets, recipes and maps are all tools that explain how to successfully reach a destination or complete a project.

In middle school, teachers often provide students with directions how to successfully complete a project. These directions are called "rubrics." A rubric is a written description of how a teacher expects a student to complete a project in order to get a good grade. A rubric sets forth the project criteria and tells the student exactly how the project will be scored. As Jamal recently discovered, the rubric is is an important tool for success in middle school:

Jamal's health class assignment was to make a poster depicting a healthy, balanced meal. His teacher, Ms. Lophat, was clear about her expectations for the poster. In fact, she even made a rubric to guide students in their poster design. Ms. Lophat gave each student in her class a copy of the rubric well in advance of the poster's due date. She also gave her students a copy of "Ms. Lophat's Rules of Rubric Road," to help them get the most out of using the rubric.

MS. LOPHAT'S RULES OF RUBRIC ROAD

3.
Read it aloud with a parent or study bud. *Pay close attention to details!*

2.
Read it!

4.
Enter the project due date in your planner.

1.
As soon as you receive a rubric (or project instructions) put it in a sheet protector in your binder.

6.
Use the rubric as a guide to plan and complete the project or assignment.

5.
Make a list of the supplies you need to complete the project.

7.
Compare your final product with the rubric to make sure you've met the criteria for a good grade!

When Jamal received the Healthy Meal Poster rubric from Ms. Lophat, he glanced at it, tossed it into his backpack and went to work on his poster. When Ms. Lophat returned the graded rubric to Jamal, he was disappointed in his scores. In five of the grading categories, he received only a *1* or *2*. Those are the lowest possible scores! He doesn't understand what he did (or didn't do) to deserve such low scores.

Ms. Lophat's Rubric for the Healthy Meal Poster Project

CRITERIA	SCORE			
The Healthy Meal Poster includes graphics or photos of a balanced and healthy meal.	④	3	2	1
Each graphic or photo of the balanced and healthy meal is labeled to identify 1) the food pictured and 2) the food group to which the food belongs.	4	3	②	1
The student attaches typewritten lab notes which include:				
• A statement of the reasons for the foods selected.	④	3	2	1
• A description of three safety procedures he/she would use when preparing the meal.	4	3	2	①
The poster includes two 3x5 unlined index cards indentifying (1) the name of a book on nutrition for teens, including the title, author, publisher and number of pages; and (2) a recipe for one of the items served in the balanced meal.	4	3	②	1
Appearance of the student's poster:				
• Poster is neat and legible.	4	3	2	①
• Uses correct grammar and spelling.	4	③	2	1
• Contains student's name, date and class period in the lower right corner.	4	3	②	1

This is Jamal's Poster:

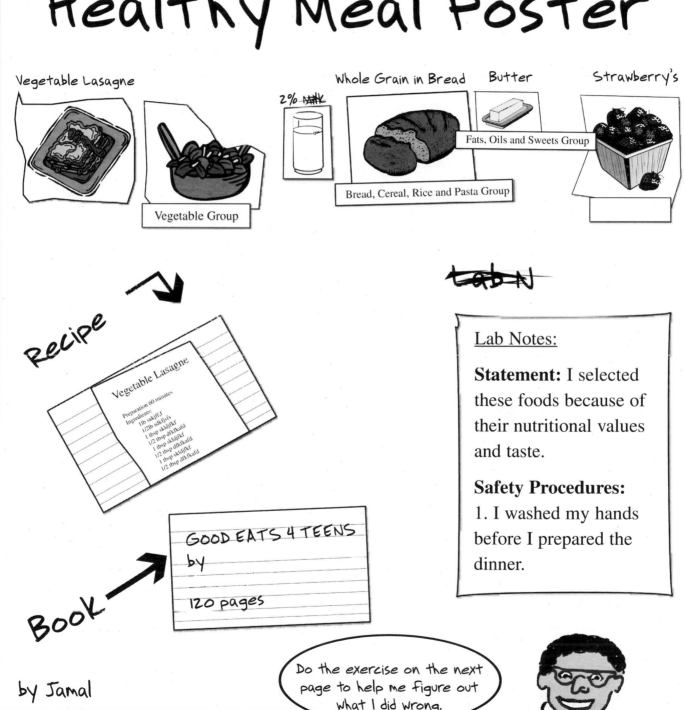

Let's Practice Middle School Work Management and Organizational Skills!

The Rubric

Compare Jamal's poster with Ms. Lophat's rubric. See if you can figure out what Jamal did (or didn't do!) on his poster to receive only 1's or 2's in five of the grading categories. Write your answers in the space provided.

The Rubric requires:	Describe how Jamal failed to follow directions:
Each of the graphics or photos is labeled to identify 1) the food pictured and 2) the food group to which the food belongs.	
A description of three safety procedures.	
Two 3x5 unlined index cards identifying the name of a book on nutrition for teens, including title, author, publisher and number of pages.	
Poster is neat and legible.	
Contains student's name, date and class period in the lower right corner.	

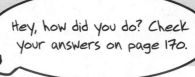

Hey, how did you do? Check your answers on page 170.

Notes:

WHAT'S NEXT?

TOOL NUMBER 8!

Tool Number 8:
The Computer

Perfect Polly thinks she's pretty good at using her computer because she can instant message, play games and send email. She also has some basic keyboarding skills. Is this enough for middle school? No! In middle school, students need to expand their knowledge of computer resources beyond IM, games, email and basic keyboarding. There are many ways to use your computer to help organize and manage your workload. From communication, to research, to tracking news and events at school, your computer is not just for games and messaging anymore! It's an important tool for success in middle school.

PERFECT POLLY PONDERS THE POSSIBILITIES:
CAN UR *CMPUTR* B 4 MOR THAN IM'S?

"Most of the stuff I was doing on my computer was just for fun—like instant messaging friends, downloading music and playing games. I never thought my computer could help me be an organized middle school student!

"Now I know that I can use my computer to communicate with my study buds, create awesome papers, find help for all sorts of homework problems, and keep up with news and events at my school.

"Using my newly-acquired computer skills, I made these cool charts to introduce you to some ways you can use your computer to help you manage and organize your work in middle school!"

Communication

Email

Communication by email is a huge time saver, especially if you're tempted to talk too long on the phone, like me!

Study Bud

Store the email addresses of your study buds in your contacts folder.

Group Project Members

Store the email addresses of your group project members in your contacts folder. Use email to remind group project members of deadlines and group meetings.

Teachers

Check with your teachers to see if it's cool to email them if you have a question about school or homework. Always put your full name and class period at the bottom of the email.

Instant Messaging

In a homework emergency, it's probably fastest to call pick up the phone and call your study bud, but have their IM info for backup! :-)

Word Processing

By the seventh grade, students should be keyboarding at least 20 to 25 words per minute. If you have a need for more speed, check your local office supply store for a good software training program. Practice just fifteen minutes a day and you'll soon be completing essays and reports much faster. Also, get familiar with these Microsoft Word features and functions to create stellar written work in middle school:

Click "Inserts" on the toolbar to access and insert these features into your paper or essay:

- page numbers
- symbols   ~ π ¢ ÷
- pictures and clipart
- organizational charts and diagrams
- shapes   ■ ● ▲

Click "Format" on the toolbar to access these features:

- fonts (size, color, style)
- paragraphs
- bullet points and numbers
- borders and shading
- colors
- document styles

Click "Tools" on the toolbar to access these helpful writing resources:

- spelling and grammar checks
- thesaurus (under "language")
- word count

Click "Table" on the toolbar to create:

- a table or graph for reports or lab journals

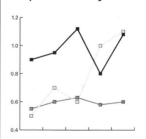

First Stop: The Middle School Tool Shed

Whether you're stuck on an algebra problem or need to know the names of the medieval capitals of Europe, help is just a click away! I made this chart to introduce you to some of my favorite homework help websites. Use the blank spaces to write the names and web addresses of *your* favorites!

Web

General Homework Help
Help for all middle school subjects:

Fact Monster Homework Center
www.factmonster.com/homework

Yahooligans!—School Bell
yahooligans.yahoo.com/school_bell/

Jishka Homework Help
www.jishka.com

Multnomah County Library Homework Center
www.multcolib.org/homework

Yahooligans! Reference
www.yahooligans.yahoo.com/reference

Name:
URL:

Name:
URL:

Name:
URL:

Math
You won't find the formula for pi in a cookbook. Check out these math websites when you need help:

Ask Dr. Math Middle School Archive
www.mathforum.org

Math.com—Homework Help
www.math.com

Webmath
www.webmath.com

Name:
URL:

Name:
URL:

Name:
URL:

Language Arts
Is your participle dangling? Do you think haiku is a martial art? These websites will help:

The Grammar Slammer
www.englishplus.com/grammar/

MS: A Language Arts Website
www.students.resa.net

Miriam-Webster Dictionary + Thesarus
www.m-w.com

IPL Teenspace A+ Writing
www.ipl.org/div/aplus

Name:
URL:

Name:
URL:

The Middle School Student's Guide to Ruling the World!

Resources

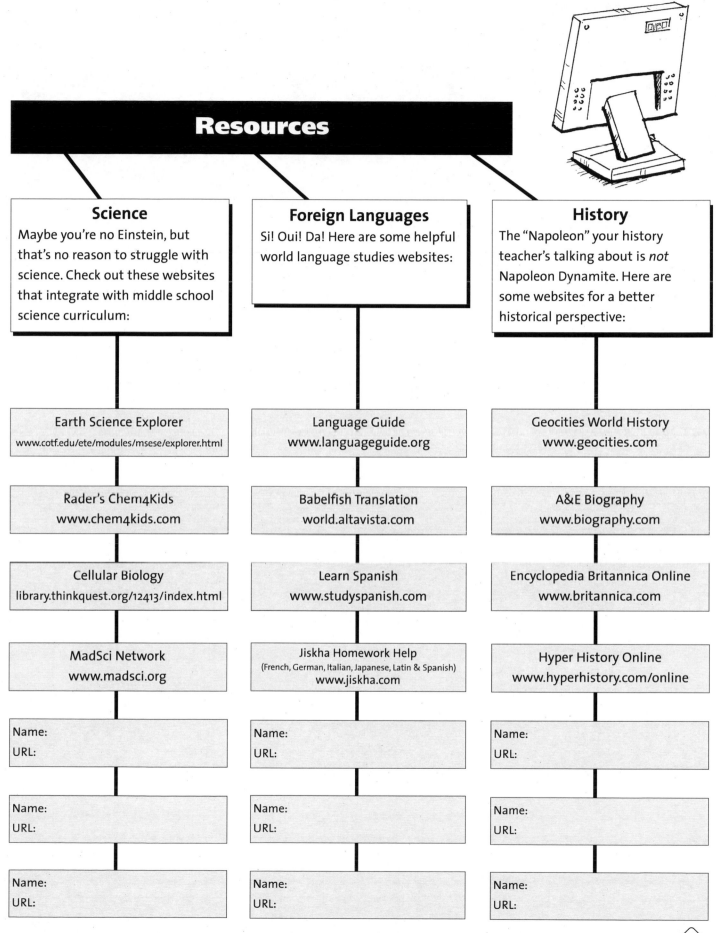

Science
Maybe you're no Einstein, but that's no reason to struggle with science. Check out these websites that integrate with middle school science curriculum:

Earth Science Explorer
www.cotf.edu/ete/modules/msese/explorer.html

Rader's Chem4Kids
www.chem4kids.com

Cellular Biology
library.thinkquest.org/12413/index.html

MadSci Network
www.madsci.org

Name:
URL:

Name:
URL:

Name:
URL:

Foreign Languages
Si! Oui! Da! Here are some helpful world language studies websites:

Language Guide
www.languageguide.org

Babelfish Translation
world.altavista.com

Learn Spanish
www.studyspanish.com

Jiskha Homework Help
(French, German, Italian, Japanese, Latin & Spanish)
www.jiskha.com

Name:
URL:

Name:
URL:

Name:
URL:

History
The "Napoleon" your history teacher's talking about is *not* Napoleon Dynamite. Here are some websites for a better historical perspective:

Geocities World History
www.geocities.com

A&E Biography
www.biography.com

Encyclopedia Britannica Online
www.britannica.com

Hyper History Online
www.hyperhistory.com/online

Name:
URL:

Name:
URL:

Name:
URL:

Back Forward Stop Refresh Home AutoFill Print Mail

Address: @

Favorites History Search Scrapbook Page Holder

Your Middle School's Website

What's up at your school? Most middle schools have websites that contain a ton of useful information to help you stay informed and organized. Here is some of the information that can be found on a typical middle school website:

Teacher's Homepage

- class schedules and calendars
- assignments and homework
- PDF reading lists, rubrics, class forms, etc.
- grades and/or links to online grades
- links to tutorial sites and helpful articles
- links to your teacher's email
- your teacher's phone number and office hours

School Administration

- policies, rules and dress codes
- school-wide schedules
- district calendars
- information for parents
- links to administrators' and counselors' email
- links to the PTA
- daily bulletin
- school newsletter
- special announcements
- map of the school

Student Activities and Services

- clubs, activities and sports
- links to club websites
- game schedules
- student government
- dance and activity permission slips
- community service information
- library information
- health services
- cafeteria services and menus
- links to and information about school approved tutors

The Middle School Student's Guide to Ruling the World!

Let's Practice Middle School Work Management and Organizational Skills!

The Computer

See if you can do better than Polly on that tech test!

Describe 10 ways you can use your computer can help you manage your middle school workload!

1.

2.

3.

4.

5.

6.

7.

8.

9.

10.

Extra credit: Write your middle school's web address here, then logon and spend some time learning to navigate the site.

_____

How did you do? Check your answers on page 171.

Notes:

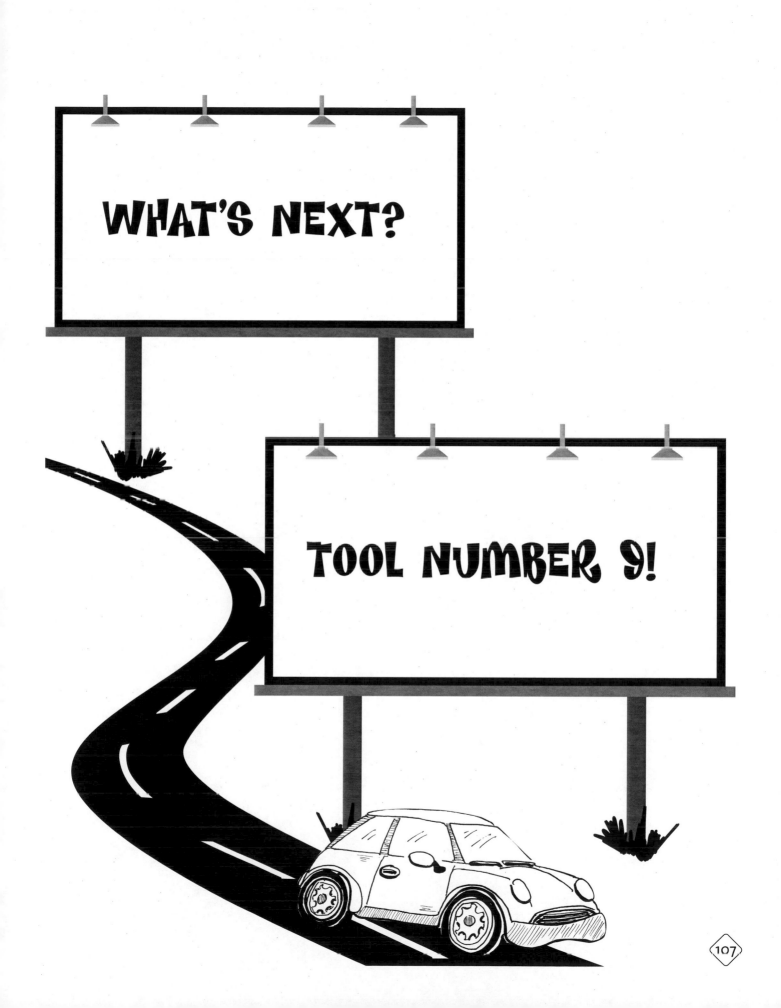

Tool Number 9: The Write Stuff

Many students blame poor grades on essays, papers and book reports on their lack of talent for writing. But did you know that low scores on written work can be the result of poor work management and organizational skills? How is this possible? What do these skills have have to do with writing? It's simple: No matter how brilliant your ideas are, or how well you understand the subject, spelling errors, boring vocabulary and poor grammar and punctuation can sink your paper's grade faster than the iceberg sank The Titanic! So before turning in written work, always take the time to use the "write tools": The dictionary, the thesaurus and a grammar & punctuation guide.

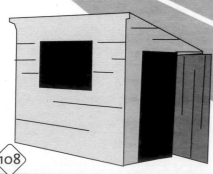

JAMAL'S ESSAY GETS AN
EXTREME MAKEOVER!

O, thou middle school student! I beseech thee to use the "write stuff."

Jamal likes his writing class, but he sure doesn't like the grades he's been getting on essays and papers. In fact, his teacher, Mr. Riteswell, recently gave Jamal his lowest score yet on his biographical essay on William Shakespeare. Now that Jamal understands that it's his responsibility to follow up on matters that affect his grade, he stops after class to talk to Mr. Riteswell about his essay.

"Hey, Mr. R, got a minute?" asks Jamal.

"Sure Jamal. What's up?"

"Well," Jamal begins, "I'd like to talk to you about the grade I got on my Shakespeare essay. Why was it so low?"

"The grade was low, Jamal," answers Mr. Riteswell, "because the essay had so many misspelled words and punctuation errors. In middle school, written work must be turned in free of spelling, grammar and punctuation errors. Also, your vocabulary wasn't sophisticated enough for a middle school student. You need to expand your vocabulary to avoid using words that are familiar and common."

"But, Mr. Riteswell!" protests Jamal, "What about my *ideas*? Can't you tell from what I wrote that my ideas are good, that I've been studying, and that I understand the subject? Isn't that enough?"

"Jamal, your ideas are excellent," Mr. Riteswell assures him, "and I'm impressed by the fact that you've stopped by today to talk to me about your grade. But good writing skills aren't just about ideas. They're also about how well your ideas are presented. In your case, that is clearly a matter of how well you manage your work!"

"What? I don't get it, Mr. Riteswell! How are my writing skills related to my *organizational* skills?"

"Think about it, Jamal," says Mr. Riteswell, "It would have taken just a few minutes of your time to correct those spelling and punctuation mistakes, and to select a better vocabulary before turning in your paper. Always keep the 'write stuff' at your work space and take the time to use these resources. They can have a significant impact on your grade!"

"The *write stuff,*' Mr. Riteswell?" asks Jamal. "I'm confused. What are you talking about?"

Before Jamal can say another word, Mr. Riteswell hands him a dictionary, a thesaurus and a grammar & punctuation guide. "Jamal," he says, "with these amazing tools and just a few minutes of your time, you can greatly improve the quality of your written work. Hey, are you up for a challenge?"

"Sure!"

"Ok. I'll give you a few minutes to use a dictionary, a thesaurus and this grammar & punctuation guide to correct your errors and give your essay an 'extreme makeover.' On your mark... get set... GO!"

Jamal opened the dictionary and quickly began working. When he finished correcting the spelling errors, he used the thesaurus to select a better vocabulary for his essay. Then he consulted the grammar & punctuation guide to correct the remaining errors. In just a few minutes, his "extreme makeover" was finished. Check it out:

BEFORE

Jamal

Language Arts and Writing

Biografical Essay Assignment – 4th Per.

Shakespear was one of the biggest and busiest writers in all of history. He wrote lots and lots of plays and a lot of sonets to. He wrote from around 1576 to 1610 I think his most important play was McBeth because it had a big influince on the english kings and queens. Shakespears most important influince was leaving behind lots of great writing that has lasted a long time.

AFTER

Jamal

Language Arts and Writing

Biographical Essay Assignment – 4th Per.

William Shakespeare was one of the most prolific writers in all of history. He wrote numerous plays and sonnets between 1576 and 1610. In my opinion, Macbeth was one of his most important plays, as it has had a substantial impact on the English monarchy. Shakespeare left a rich and enduring legacy to the world.

"So, Jamal," says Mr. Riteswell, "you can see that both essays contain the same basic facts and ideas, right?"

"Right!"

"By taking the time and using the 'write stuff,' you've eliminated misspelled words, punctuation and grammar errors, and boring vocabulary. Congratulations, Jamal!" says Mr. Ritewell as he marks an *A* on Jamal's paper, "In just a few minutes, your essay has gone from fair to *fantastic*!"

THE DICTIONARY

Count on it! Teachers always catch spelling mistakes, so review your written work for spelling mistakes before turning it in. The fastest and easiest way to avoid misspelling words is to use a dictionary. If you're not sure how to spell a word, don't guess. Look it up!

THE THESUARUS

Middle school teachers want students to expand their vocabularies and move away from using familiar and common words in writing. The easiest way to do this is to use a *thesaurus*. A thesaurus is a book of words and their synonyms. Finding more descriptive words for essays and reports is easy. They're right in the thesaurus! Keep a thesaurus at your workspace. It takes only a minute to use, but it can have a huge, great, immense, enormous, vast, gigantic and massive impact on your grade!

THE PUNCTUATION AND GRAMMAR GUIDE

Avoid punctuation and grammar errors by using a punctuation and grammar guide. Here are some good ones that can be purchased at any major bookstore, or online through Amazon.com:

• *Painless Grammar*, by Rebecca Elliot. This is written for sixth through eighth graders.

• *Webster's New World Student Writing Handbook, 4th Ed.*, by Sharon Sorenson. Right to the point!

• *English Simplified, 10th Ed.*, by Blanch Ellsworth and John A. Higgins. This one fits into your binder for easy reference.

TIP: USE YOUR COMPUTER TO CHECK SPELLING.

In Microsoft Word, access your computer's spell check function by clicking "tools" on the tool bar. Scroll down to "Spelling and Grammar" and click. The correct spelling will appear in the box. When keyboarding a paper, essay or report, always do a spelling and grammar check before printing the final version. For a good online dictionary go to Merriam-Webster online dictionary at www.m-w.com.

TIP: USE YOUR COMPUTER TO IMPROVE VOCABULARY.

In Microsoft Word, the thesaurus function can be accessed by right-clicking on the first letter of the word that you want to look up. Scroll down to "synonym," and various word choices will pop up. Click on a word, and it is automatically inserted into your sentence. You can also access the thesaurus function from the tool bar at the top of your screen. Click on "tools," scroll down to "language" and then to "thesaurus." For a good online thesaurus, go to Merriam-Webster online thesaurus at www.m-w.com.

The Middle School Student's Guide to Ruling the World!

Let's Practice Middle School Work Management and Organizational Skills!

The Write Stuff

Use your dictionary, thesaurus, and a grammar & punctuation guide to give this essay an extreme makeover. Record your time below. On your mark... get set... GO!

BEFORE

There are lots of different kinds of writing. There is nonfickshon and fisckshon like science historical and realistic. Any good story makes people want to read it. There are some really old stories written by guys like Plato and Arisdotel that tell us about the really old times and what people did and how they lived. Some science fiskshon stories are set in a time way far ahead. They tell what life will be like a long time from now.

AFTER

Start: _____

Finish: _____

Time to complete makeover:

_____

How did you do? Check your answers on page 171.

Notes:

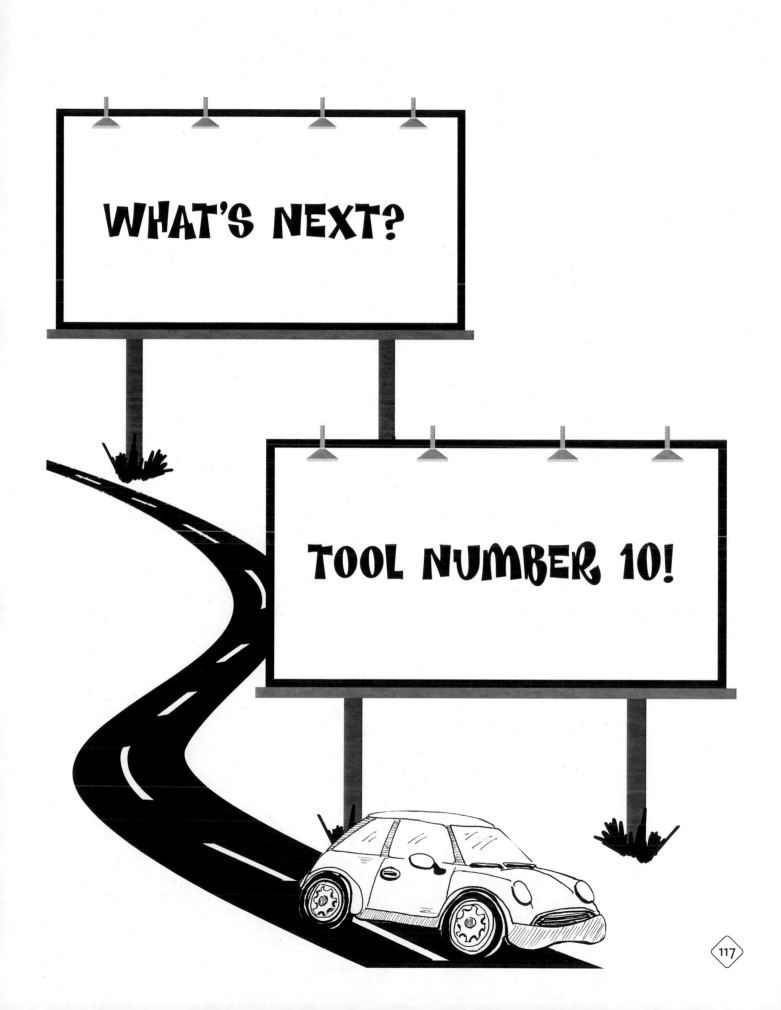

Tool Number 10:
The Mental Checklist

One of the best habits you can develop to help you manage and organize your middle school workload is to <u>think</u> about it. The great thing about thinking is that you can do it anytime and anywhere. It requires no special materials or supplies, other than the head on your shoulders! So many middle school students walk around like zombies, barely thinking for themselves, expecting teachers or parents to think for them. Like Polly, they rely on others to keep track of their responsibilities, and sometimes blame others when they make mistakes or forget things. If this sounds like you, stop taking a free ride on somebody else's brain and think for yourself! In this chapter you will learn how to create your very own "Mental Checklist" – an excellent tool for being organized in middle school!

POLLY EXPERIENCES THE AMAZING POWERS OF THE MENTAL CHECKLIST

OR

"WHAT TO DO WHEN YOUR BRAIN GOES ON VACATION WITHOUT YOU"

Unless her mom reminded her, Polly would often forget to bring her homework to school. She'd also forget her lunch money and permission slips. She could never remember to return library books. Last semester she lost her gym shoes once and her bus pass twice. Sometimes she felt like her brain had gone on vacation without the rest of her!

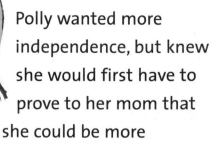

Polly wanted more independence, but knew she would first have to prove to her mom that she could be more responsible. Polly wasn't sure she could do it. Then, at the Middle School Tool Shed, she experienced an awesome and amazing power. It is the power of the Mental Checklist and it has changed her life!

Dear Polly,
Having a great time!
Wish you were here!

Love,
Brainy

The Middle School Student's Guide to Ruling the World!

"What's a Mental Checklist? It's simple! A Mental Checklist is a thinking survey of the day ahead of you. You do it every morning before leaving for school. A Mental Checklist really helps forgetful students (like me) remember to bring to school all of the homework, books and stuff they need for the day—without having to be reminded! Since I started using my Mental Checklist, I no longer forget things and lose stuff, like I used to."

Making a Mental Checklist is as easy as 1-2-3-4! Here's how:

1

A Mental Checklist is done at the *same* time and in the *same* place every morning before leaving for school. I do my Mental Checklist when I'm brushing my teeth. My friend Sara does her Mental Checklist when she's eating breakfast. Jamal does his when he's packing his backpack.

2

As soon as I start brushing my teeth, I clear my mind. I focus on the day ahead of me.

3

I ask myself these questions *every* morning:

- Is my homework in my binder?

- Are my binders in my backpack?

- Have I packed everything I need for the day? (Lunch? Planner? Gym clothes? Bus Pass?)

- Do I have any special responsibilities today? (Permission slips? Return library book? Schedule changes?)

4

If I have forgotten something, I take care of it right away, before I forget it again!

"OK, now get this! The key to making a Mental Checklist that works is consistency. Try to follow the *same* thought pattern at the *same* time and in the *same* place every day. Make it a *habit*! It may take a couple of weeks to get used to doing your Mental Checklist, but it's a skill that you can use all of your life to help you stay organized, so it's worth giving it a good try.

"I also do a Mental Checklist at my locker every afternoon before I leave school for home. It helps me remember to bring home all of the books, worksheets and binders I need for homework."

The Middle School Student's Guide to Ruling the World!

Do
Mental
Checklist

TIP:

At first, it may help to post a note to remind you to begin your Mental Checklist. Once you make your Mental Checklist a daily habit, you'll be amazed how much you can remember without having to be reminded! (You can also go to www.middleschoolguide.com to download and print your Mental Checklist reminder.)

First Stop: The Middle School Tool Shed

Let's Practice Middle School Work Management and Organizational Skills!

The Mental Checklist

Do you sometimes forget to bring your homework to school? Do you forget to return library books or lose things? Have you forgotten your lunch too many times? If so, it's your turn to go totally mental! Here's how:

First, decide what activity you'll use to begin your Mental Checklist. Pick an activity you do every morning at about the same time and in the same place. List the things you need to remember to do. Make your Mental Checklist a *daily habit*!

_____ 'S MENTAL CHECKLIST

I will do my Mental Checklist every morning when I am:

_____.

These are the things I need to remind myself to do before I leave for school.

✔ _____

✔ _____

✔ _____

✔ _____

✔ _____

Notes:

STOP

NEXT STOP:
THE HOMEWORK
DETECTIVE AGENCY!

The Homework Detective Agency

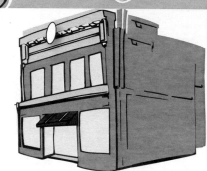

Welcome to the second stop on the journey to success in middle school: The Homework Detective Agency! You've come a long way, but the journey's not over. Now that you've learned all about the tools you need to be an organized middle school student, it's time to consider your work habits – specifically, your homework habits.

Most students will agree that doing homework is hard and not much fun. But is it possible that bad homework habits are making you work harder than you need to? Good homework habits are easy to learn, and since you have to do your homework (yes, you _do_ have to do it), doesn't it make sense to develop habits that will help you to do your best work in the least amount of time? Let's see what you know about homework habits. Tag along with Detective Ace Bandich as he investigates unsolved homework crimes and mysteries...

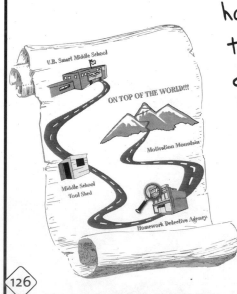

Second Stop: The Homework Detective Agency

On the Case with Ace

Case No. 1: THE CASE OF THE
NASTY HOMEWORK HABITS

It's mid-afternoon when you arrive at the Homework Detective Agency. You make your way to the second floor and down the dim lit hall to the office of Ace Bandich. The sign on the door tells you that you're in the right place.

> OFFICE OF
> **ACE BANDICH**
>
> STAR INVESTIGATOR OF
> UNSOLVED HOMEWORK CRIMES
> AND MYSTERIES

As soon as you walk in, Ace looks up, smiles and tosses a file your way. "Hey, kid!" he says, "Welcome aboard! I've been waiting for you. Take a look at this case. It's really got me puzzled. Let's see if we can solve it right away."

Always up for a challenge, you open the file and begin to read...

The Middle School Student's Guide to Ruling the World!

CASE INFORMATION

Larry, middle school student

Subject's Name:

Late Larry.

Background Information:

Subject is a student at U.B. Smart Middle School. No matter how hard he tries, he can't stay on top of his homework. It takes him hours to finish. Sometimes he never finishes! His mother, Mad Mary, is fed up with his homework habits. She has hired the Homework Detective Agency to detect and correct Larry's nasty homework habits.

Problem:

Subject can't manage his homework load.

Recommendation:

Investigate. Observe subject's homework habits. Figure out why he isn't getting his homework done.

Surveillance is recommended.

Scene of suspected Homework Crime

Suspect's mother, Mad Mary

Later that day...

You're on the case with Ace! You've followed Larry home from school and set up a homework "stake out":

3:50 p.m. Begin surveillance. Subject (Larry) arrives home from school and stops in the kitchen for a snack. He consumes a bag of chips, a half-dozen cookies, a donut and two sodas.

4:20 p.m.: Subject belches loudly and proceeds from kitchen to the desk in his room. He begins doing homework.

4:30: Subject takes a break in the middle of an assignment. He proceeds to the family room where he is observed playing a video game against his little brother, Lazy Lonnie. Subject takes a pounding but continues to play... and play... and play...

5:45: Finally winning a game, subject proceeds (triumphantly) to his room to continue his homework. Subject makes a stop at the hall bathroom and is observed entering with his favorite comic book.

5:55: Subject remains in hall bathroom...

6:05: Subject still in bathroom...

6:10: Subject exits bathroom (with comic book) and proceeds to his room where he continues doing homework.

6:30: Subject's mother calls him for dinner. He leaves his room and goes to the kitchen..

6:58: Subject finishes dinner and heads back to his room to complete his homework. On the way, he stops in the family room and appears to enter a trance-like state in front of the television.

The Middle School Student's Guide to Ruling the World!

Surveillance continued...

7:30: Subject finishes watching a t.v. show and begins to watch another. Subject's mother begins to question him as to whether he's finished his homework. She is suspicious.

8:00: Subject heads to his room to continue homework. He selects some music, puts on headphones, cranks up the volume and begins to work.

9:00: Subject closes his books and appears to have completed his homework. Subject hangs out in his room doing nothing.

9:30: Subject suddenly panics. It appears that he has forgotten about a book report that is due the next day. His mother, Mad Mary enters his room and tells him to go to bed. Subject explains that he has not completed the book report. Mad Mary lives up to her name.

9:35: Subject begins book report...

9:50: Subject writing book report...

10:00: Still writing book report...

10:35: Subject's eyelids are drooping.

10:45: Subject is asleep at his desk. The book report is not finished.

10:46: Surveillance ends.

Let's Practice Middle School Work Management and Organizational Skills!

Detect, Correct and Solve: The Case of the Nasty Homework Habits

1. Larry consumed a lot of junk food when he got home from school. Can an unhealthy diet affect his ability to learn, remember and stay alert while doing homework?

   a. Yes, absolutely!

   b. No, healthy food is over-rated.

   c. Food has nothing to do with learning, remembering and staying alert.

   d. I have no idea.

2. Larry takes a lot of study breaks. His breaks seem to last a long time because he gets distracted by video games, comic books and television. What's wrong?

   a. Nothing. Taking up to 6 hours to finish a normal middle school homework load is perfectly fine.

   b. Larry should put a television in his room so that he can do his homework and watch t.v. at the same time. That way he would take fewer breaks.

   c. Larry's breaks are too long for the amount of time he has actually worked.

   d. None of the above.

3. Larry listens to music while doing homework. In fact, he's downloaded hundreds of songs onto his iPod®. He thinks that listening to music while he studies keeps him from getting bored. Which style of music is better for him to do homework to?

   a. Rock

   b. Rap

   c. Hip-Hop

   d. None of the above.

4. Larry starts and stops homework in the middle of assignments. He is easily distracted by non-homework matters. He has no plan for doing his homework and he forgets assignments (like book reports). What is a "homework routine" and why is it important for a student like Larry?

   a. A homework routine is a song and dance that inspires students to keep working.

   b. A homework routine is a plan for doing homework at the same time, and in a consistent manner every day.

   c. A homework routine is nothing Larry needs to worry about until he is in high school.

   d. I have no idea what a homework routine is, and routines bore me.

5. Larry wasted a lot of time today. If he had taken shorter breaks and avoided distractions, he would have had enough time to finish his book report. He would also have had some free time and gotten to bed on time. Why is it important for Larry to tackle his homework earlier in the day?

   a. A student's efficiency drops later in the evening.

   b. Finishing earlier will allow him time to relax and do some fun stuff.

   c. He would have had time to handle unanticipated problems, delays or emergencies.

   d. All of the above

Hey kid, how'd you do? Compare your detective skills with mine on page 133.

DETECTIVE ACE SOLVES
The Case of the Nasty Homework Habits

1. Studies have shown that foods differ greatly in their effects on the brain's ability to process information, retain facts and stay alert. Different foods create different chemical reactions in the brain. Foods that are high in sugar provide a brief boost in energy, but ultimately slow down the brain's ability to process information. A diet that is higher in protein boosts the brain's ability to work efficiently. If Larry wants to do a better job on homework and finish faster, he should dump his soda n' donut diet in favor of snacks like cheese, fruit, milk or a healthy sandwich. **Answer: A.**

2. Larry drags out the homework process far longer than necessary, because he does not work steadily or efficiently. His two so-called "breaks" totaled more than three hours! The rule of thumb for a middle school student is *one 5 minute break for every 30 minutes of homework*. Before taking a break, Larry should complete the assignment he's working on, and set up for the next, by taking out his paper and opening his text book to the correct page. When he returns from his break, he should begin working immediately and *keep his rear in the chair!*
Answer: C.

3. Sorry Larry, but study after study has proven that the sounds of tv, radio, music or people talking will distract the brain from learning no matter how much a student enjoys it or how much

they claim to be used to it. If Larry truly wants to finish his homework sooner *and* do a better job—he should limit his listening time to his breaks. **Answer: D.**

4. Regarding good homework habits, consistency is key! Larry needs to develop a homework routine and stick to it. As much as possible, he should do his homework at the same time and in the same place every day. At homework time, he should go to directly his work space, check his planner for assignments and proceed through each of his classes, completing homework in a consistent order. **Answer: B.**

5. Once and awhile every student, even an organized one, has to stay up late to finish homework or complete a project. It's just a fact of life when you're balancing school, sports and a social life. But it's important that it doesn't happen too often. Studies have shown that a student's efficiency drops later in the evening. That means it will take Larry longer to finish his report and he'll probably not do as good a job as he would have, if he'd started earlier in the day. If he's tired and sleepy, he should go to sleep! Sleep has been proven to help absorb information that has been reviewed. Finishing homework before school is ok, provided he gets up early enough to complete the work, eat breakfast and be on time for school.
Answer: D.

SARA'S BEEN ACTING A LITTLE ODD LATELY. SHE THINKS SHE'S BEING FOLLOWED...

SLAM!

AGGHHH!!!

TO BE CONTINUED...

The Middle School Student's Guide to Ruling the World!

What's Stalking the Students of U.B. Smart Middle School?

Case No. 2: THE CASE OF THE
SNEAKY SOCIAL STUDIES PROJECT

You and Ace congratulate yourselves on solving the Case of the Nasty Homework Habits and head back to the Homework Detective Agency. The phone rings as soon as you walk in the door. It's Scattered Sara. She sounds terrified! You can barely make out what she's saying... something about a "social studies project" and "out of control." Ace tells her to sit tight—you're on the way!

When you and Ace arrive at Sara's house, you find her huddled in a corner of her room, muttering about her project being "late" and "a total mess." Once you get her to calm down, she tells you the whole, horrible story:

"Lately," she begins, "I've been feeling kind of nervous and uneasy—like something's sneaking up on me! I haven't been able to figure out what it is, and I can't shake the feeling. It stays with me most of the day. It's especially bad at night, when I'm doing homework. Suddenly, I realized what it is! It's my social studies project! It's been sneaking up on me for weeks and now it's out of control! It's due in two days! I've hardly done any of the work. I haven't finished the research. I haven't got any of the supplies I need. Ace, what happened? How did this all get so crazy?!" Sara dissolves into sobs. Ace frowns and shakes his head. "Unfortunately, Sara," he says, "it sounds like you were never warned about a dangerous creature that stalks unsuspecting middle school students. This creature has been known to sneak up on them, turn their lives into chaos and vanish, only to return again and again during the school year! It strikes fear in the hearts of even the best students. It's known as the:

AGGHHH!!!

Long Term Project!

WARNING! SPECIAL BULLETIN CONCERNING THREAT TO MIDDLE SCHOOL STUDENTS

- **NAME:** Long Term Project   **ALIASES:** "Book Report," "Class Project," "Science Project" "Essay" and similar assignments.

- **DESCRIPTION:** The Long Term Project can be identified by its due date. It is always due more than one day from the date it was assigned.

- **TAKE CONTROL:** Take control of the Long Term Project immediately. Circle in your planner the date the Long Term Project is due and, beginning with the day *before*, count backward to the date it was assigned. That is how many days you have to complete the Long Term Project.

- **READ THE DIRECTIONS:** You are strongly advised to read and then *reread* your teacher's directions for the Long Term Project. (**Tip:** Follow the Rules of Rubric Road.)

SELECT A PLAN FOR COMPLETING THE LONG TERM PROJECT:

PLAN A:	PLAN B:	PLAN C:
The "Split and Tackle" Plan	**The "Chunk and Block" Plan**	**The "Wait 'til the Last Minute" Plan**
(1) Carefully review the Project Directions or Rubric;	(1) Carefully review the Project Directions or Rubric.	Although popular with many students, Plan C is *not* an option in middle school.
(2) Split the Long Term Project into several smaller projects or tasks;	(2) Organize the Long Term Project into "chunks" of work that can logically be completed at the same time, such as research at the local library on several issues.	
(3) Write each task in your planner;	(3) "Block" enough time in your planner (sometimes several hours) after school or on weekends;	
(4) Tackle one or more task each day, *as part of your normal homework routine*, until the project is finished.	(4) Work on the "chunks" of the project until it is finished.	

CAUTION: Make a list of supplies needed to complete the project. **Do not wait until the last minute to ask parents to obtain supplies.**

SPECIAL PROJECT FOLDER: Separate your Long Term Project materials from other school papers, and keep them in a special project folder or binder.

"Ace," says Sara, "now I know that the best way of controlling a Long Term Project is to know how many days I have to get the project done *and* have a plan for completing it!"

"That's right, Sara" says Ace.

"When my teacher assigns a Long Term Project, I immediately mark the due date in my planner. I figure out the number of days I have to complete the project. I follow the Rules of Rubric Road and read (and reread) the directions. Then I make a plan for getting the work done!"

"Right!" says Ace.

"I make a list of all of the supplies I need, and give it to my mom or dad. I make a special folder to hold my Long Term Project materials like rough drafts, research and handouts. After that, I get working! No more 'Wait 'til the Last Minute Plan' for me!"

"Bingo. You got it, Sara! Consider this case closed!"

How to Get Control of the Long Term Project:

1. Mark the due date in your planner.

2. Count the days until the project is due;

3. Read and *reread* the rubric or project instructions;

4. Make a "Split and Tackle" or a "Chunk and Block" plan for completing the project. Write the plan tasks in your planner.

5. Keep your project materials in a special folder.

6. Get working according to the plan!

Second Stop: The Homework Detective Agency

Let's Practice Middle School Work Management and Organizational Skills!

Detect, Correct and Solve:
The Case of the Sneaky Social Studies Project

Here's a blank page from Sara's planner. Help her complete her Social Studies Long Term Project on time by creating a "Split and Tackle Plan," or a "Chunk and Block Plan." Make a list of the supplies she'll need to finish her project. Today is Monday the 10th. The project is due on Friday the 21st.

SOCIAL STUDIES LONG TERM PROJECT

Write a 300 word essay about Franklin Delano Roosevelt's New Deal, responding to the following prompt: In your opinion, what was the most effective program of the New Deal?

Support your essay with facts that you have learned from researching the program you select. Using colored pencils or markers and an 11"x17" poster board, create a campaign poster that features the highlights of your New Deal Program. Put your name and class period on the back of the poster on a 3"x5" index card. Prepare a 3 minute speech persuading the class that the program you selected was the most effective of the New Deal.

Monday 10	Tuesday 11	Wednesday 12	Thursday 13	Friday 14	Sat/Sun 15/16
Monday 17	Tuesday 18	Wednesday 19	Thursday 20	**Friday 21**	Sat/Sun 22/23

Dear Mom or Dad:

I need these supplies for my social studies project:

1.

2.

3.

4.

I need the supplies by _____.

Thanks!

Sara

Hey kid. How'd you do? Compare your detective skills with mine on page 172.

Notes:

Case No. 3:
THE MYSTERY OF THE
MISSING HOMEWORK ASSIGNMENTS

Chris receives a Mysterious Note

Back at the Homework Detective Agency, Ace has another client waiting. It's Chronically Disorganized Chris and he's looking pretty worried. He's got reason to be. He's missing some very valuable items: three homework assignments! He had no idea they were missing until he received this mysterious note from his math teacher:

Name of Student: **Chris**

Problem: **Missing Homework Assignments**

Date of Assignment:	Item:
2/5	Math journal entry
3/22	Workbook pages 223–225
3/25	Chapter 6 problems 40–56

You have 2 days to turn in the missing assignments in order to receive credit.

Yours Truly,

Ms. Meanmode, Your Math Teacher

Chris wants Ace to track down the missing assignments, but Ace suspects that something's wrong. Before hitting the pavement in search of the rogue reports, he fires some questions at Chris:

"Chris, have you been using your planner to keep track of assignments? Have you been listening in class for homework changes and new assignments? Have you been putting your homework in your binder?!"

"Yes, yes and more yes!" Chris insists. "I'm trying to do all those things, but, I admit that I *am* having problems with classes like math and science, where there are so many different types of homework assignments to keep track of. There's journaling, textbook assignments, handouts, workbook pages, lab books, research, chapter outlines, vocabulary flashcards, essays, projects... It goes on and on and on. Sometimes I get confused and lose track of what I need to do!"

Ace considers Chris's story, then asks, "Chris, is it possible that these assignments aren't really missing? Is it possible that they were never completed at all, or that you misplaced them?"

A confused look crosses Chris's face, then suddenly his eyes widen. He jumps out of his chair excitedly. "You're right, Ace! You've solved the mystery. Those assignments aren't lost! Two of them are 'missing' because I forgot to do them. The other one is still on my desk at home because I forgot to put it in my binder!" Relieved, Chris thanks Ace, shakes his hand and turns to leave.

"Hold it one minute, Chris! Not so fast." Ace says, "This case isn't solved yet."

"Huh? I don't get it, Ace. I hired you to track down the missing assignments and since they aren't really missing, your job is done."

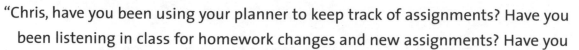

Ace puts a hand on Chris's shoulder, "Chris, my friend, if I let you walk out of here right now, you'll be back again next week, and the week after, and the week after that, always with the same problem."

The Middle School Student's Guide to Ruling the World!

"What are you talking about?"

"I'm talking about really solving this case. I'm talking about setting you up so that you'll never forget to do any part of your homework, or leave it at home again."

"Man, I'm *in*! But, *how*?" Chris listens as Ace explains...

Ace Lets Chris in on a Secret

"Chris, I am going let you in on a little secret. It's called 'The Homework Tracking Chart.'"

"The Homework *what*?!" Chris asks.

"The Homework Tracking Chart," says Ace. "Let me explain. The Homework Tracking Chart is a personalized chart that helps you keep track of all of the different types of homework you could have in any class. It is especially useful for classes that have a large variety of homework assignments. For example, you have lots of different types of homework in science, right? There's textbook reading, vocabulary flashcards, lab book work, research, workbook pages, reports, chapter outlines, studying for quizzes... It's doubtful that your teacher would ever assign all of the different types of homework for a single night. But a quick glance at your Homework Tracking Chart will prompt you to consider it all, so that you forget nothing! It also prompts you to put your homework in your binder, so that it gets to school the next day."

"Cool!"

"The Homework Tracking Chart takes only a few minutes to make. Post it at your workspace. It will guide you to approach homework in an organized and consistent manner every day. That will help you establish a homework *routine*, and we all know that having a homework routine minimizes the risk that you'll overlook an assignment or misplace your homework."

"Ace! You're a genius! How do I create this thing you call 'The Homework Tracking Chart'?"

"In five easy steps, my man, just five easy steps!"

ACE'S 5 EASY STEPS FOR MAKING A PERSONAL HOMEWORK TRACKING CHART

1. Make a chart with one column for each of your classes.

2. Label each column with the name of a class (the order of classes doesn't matter).

3. Under each class, write "Check Planner," since checking your planner for assignments is the first thing you should do when you start homework. If your teacher posts homework to the class website, you need to include a reminder to check it too.

4. Going class by class, brainstorm (that means think really hard about) and list all of the types of homework that could be assigned for that class.

5. Finish each list with a binder prompt, to remind you to always put your finished homework in your binder. Post your Homework Tracking Chart at your workspace, where you can see it.

The Middle School Student's Guide to Ruling the World!

Chris's Homework Tracking Chart

Math

- Check planner
- Check class website
- Workbook pages/problems
- Textbook pages/problems
- Math journal entry
- Study for quiz/test
- Homework in binder?

Language Arts

- Check planner
- Workbook pages
- Journaling
- Assigned reading
- Homework in binder?

Science

- Check planner
- Check class website
- Worksheet problems
- Textbook reading
- Vocabulary flashcards
- Lab book work
- Handout reading
- Outline chapters
- Study for test/quiz
- Long Term Project work
- Homework in binder?

History

- Check planner
- Check class website
- Reading: Textbook
- Reading: Handouts
- Answer textbook questions
- Study for test/quiz
- Long term project work
- Homework in binder?

Spanish

- Check planner
- Workbook pages
- Vocabulary flashcards
- Study for quiz
- Homework in binder?

Health

- Check planner
- Assigned reading
- Long Term Project work
- Homework in binder?

Let's Practice Middle School Work Management and Organizational Skills!

Complete the Homework Tracking Chart to solve the mystery of <u>your</u> missing assignments!

Here's a blank Homework Tracking Chart. List your classes, then list all of the different types of homework that could be assigned in that class. Post the Homework Tracking Chart at your workspace. Update it whenever a different type of homework is introduced. (You can also go to www.middleschoolguide.com to download and print as many Homework Tracking Charts as you need!)

Class: _____	Class: _____	Class: _____
• Check planner	• Check planner	• Check planner
• _____	• _____	• _____
• _____	• _____	• _____
• _____	• _____	• _____
• _____	• _____	• _____
• _____	• _____	• _____
• _____	• _____	• _____
• Homework in binder?	• Homework in binder?	• Homework in binder?
Class: _____	Class: _____	Class: _____
• Check planner	• Check planner	• Check planner
• _____	• _____	• _____
• _____	• _____	• _____
• _____	• _____	• _____
• _____	• _____	• _____
• _____	• _____	• _____
• _____	• _____	• _____
• Homework in binder?	• Homework in binder?	• Homework in binder?

Notes:

STOP

NEXT STOP: MOTIVATION MOUNTAIN!

Motivation Mountain

At last, you have reached the foot of Motivation Mountain! Your journey to success in middle school is nearly complete. You're using the tools you need to organize and manage your workload. You've conquered nasty homework habits. You've established a consistent and productive homework routine. But do you know that these things will take you only part of the way to success? Ultimately, your success is dependent upon a powerful force that only <u>you</u> can generate:

MOTIVATION!

How do you get motivated to succeed in middle school? Find out right here on Motivation Mountain!

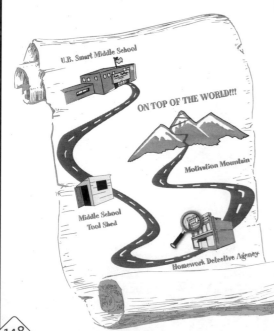

The Middle School Student's Guide to Ruling the World!

Hello, I am Bob, guru of middle school goals. I will be your guide to the top of Motivation Mountain. Here are your instructions:

THE QUEST: Climb Motivation Mountain to discover the secrets to success in middle school.

THE METHOD: There are eight levels. At each level you will encounter a challenge in the form of a question. Guru Bob will answer the question to reveal part of the secret to success in middle school.

MASTERY: Demonstrate mastery of the challenge question by completing a brief exercise, then advance to the next level. Complete the last and most difficult challenge, and you will advance to top of Motivation Mountain, where you will Rule the World!

CHEATS AND ANSWERS PROVIDED

SAMPLE CHALLENGE QUESTIONS

- What do goals have to do with motivation in middle school?
- What is a goalbuster?
- Can a bad attitude hurt your grade?

SAMPLE SILLY QUESTIONS

- Should vegetarians eat animal crackers?
- Why can't you breathe through your nose and your mouth at the same time?
- What would happen if everyone in the world flushed their toilet at the same time?

Third Stop: Motivation Mountain

What is a goal, and why are goals important to motivation in middle school?

"Goals? Hey, Guru Bob, I know about goals. The 'goal' of my football team is to win the game. By keeping the goal in mind, we are able to battle through four hard quarters, even though we're tired and sometimes taking a pounding from the other team. We are motivated to work hard because we want to achieve our goal of winning. Yeah! Go Fighting Owls!"

Goals are important for school, too!

GURU BOB'S ANSWER:

"Exactly, Larry. A goal is something you want to achieve! Goals are important, because when you really want something, you are motivated to work hard to get it. Goals are not just for sports—they're important for school too. Setting goals for middle school is one of the best things you can do to ensure your success. Having goals will help you stay motivated to work hard to keep up your new organizational skills."

The Middle School Student's Guide to Ruling the World!

Think about a time in your life, in school, sports or any other activity, when you wanted to achieve something. Describe the goal and what you did to achieve it.

My goal (what I wanted to achieve):

_____

_____

What I did to achieve my goal:

_____

_____

_____

_____

_____

CHEAT

Stuck on the Level One Challenge? Can't think of a time you set a goal and worked to achieve it? Here's a cheat:

There are many ways to demonstrate mastery of this challenge. Have you ever practiced hard to improve in a sport? Studied to improve your spelling or math test scores? Played a musical instrument? Done chores to earn money to buy something you wanted? If so, you had a goal! Describe any effort you made, or action you took to achieve the goal (whether you succeeded or not!) If you cannot think of a time you've set a goal and worked to achieve it, think of a goal you have for the future and what you plan to do to achieve it.

Check your answers on page 172.

YOU MAY ADVANCE TO LEVEL TWO →

Level 2 Challenge:

What goals should a student have for middle school?

"I have a goal for middle school! I want to do well. Isn't that a good goal?"

GURU BOB'S ANSWER:

"It's a start, Polly, but goals for middle school should be more than just a general desire to do well. Everyone wants to do well in school, even those kids who claim not to care! Goals should be *specific*. Successful athletes set clear and measurable goals, such as a time for finishing a race or the achievement of a certain score. Clear goals make it easier to measure progress and achievement. Having a goal for the grade you want to earn in each of your classes will help you keep track of your progress. It also makes the goal more real to you.

"Setting a grade goal is easy. Your goal should be to get the grade you would expect to receive for making your best effort in the class. 'Best effort' means using all of your new organizational skills, keeping up with homework, reading and projects, participating in class and studying for tests and quizzes. In subjects that are more difficult for you, 'best effort' may also mean putting in some extra time studying, asking for help from your teacher, or doing extra credit when it's offered."

Make your best effort in every class!

The Middle School Student's Guide to Ruling the World!

List 10 things you can do to make your best effort in a class:

1. _____

2. _____

3. _____

4. _____

5. _____

6. _____

7. _____

8. _____

9. _____

10. _____

CHEAT

Stuck on the Level Two Challenge? Here's a cheat:

Making your best effort means using all of the tools and skills you have learned about in ***The Middle School Student's Guide to Ruling the World!*** It also means keeping up with homework, reading and projects, participating in class, studying for tests and quizzes, and following up on matters that affect your grade. Some subjects will be harder for you than others, and may require more effort on your part. Remember—making your best effort also means asking for help when you need it.

Check your answers on page 173.

YOU MAY ADVANCE TO LEVEL THREE ➜

What is Goaldilock's Rule of Goal Setting?

"Last semester my report card wasn't very good. I barely made *C*'s! I was unhappy with my grades and my parents were disappointed. They knew I could do better. To make up for my report card, I promised to get straight *A*'s on the next one. When the report card came, my grades had improved, but I didn't get anywhere near the straight *A*'s I had promised. I was discouraged and my parents were disappointed again. I felt like giving up. What went wrong?"

GURU BOB'S ANSWER:

"Sara, achieving goals takes patience and time! It wasn't reasonable for you to set your goals so high for the very next semester. Goals are achieved in small steps, not in giant leaps. Aiming for some *B*'s would have been more reasonable. After reaching your goals, you would have had the confidence to set them higher the next semester. Setting goals too high is a sure way to fail and lose confidence, which can cause you to lose your motivation.

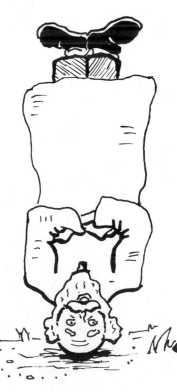

"Did you know that setting goals that are too low can be just as discouraging as setting goals that are too high? Goals should challenge you! There is nothing challenging about doing what you know you are already capable of doing. Reaching a goal that requires too little effort does nothing to build the self-confidence or the self-discipline you need to succeed in middle school.

"Follow Goaldilock's Rule of Goal Setting."

Goals shouldn't be too easy. Goals shouldn't be too hard. They should be juuuuust right!

The Middle School Student's Guide to Ruling the World!

1. Goals are achieved in small steps, not in giant leaps, so achieving your goals takes
_____ and _____ .

2. Setting goals too high is a sure way to _____ and lose _____ .

3. Setting goals that are too _____ is just as discouraging as setting goals that are too high.

4. There is nothing challenging about _____

_____ .

5. The Goaldilocks Rule of Goal Setting says that your goals shouldn't be too _____ and they shouldn't be too _____ . They should be _____ _____ !

CHEAT

Stuck on the Level Three Challenge? Here's a cheat: Reread page 156 !

Check your answers on page 173.

YOU MAY ADVANCE TO LEVEL FOUR ➜

What about activity and interest goals in middle school?

"Middle school is so different from elementary school. There are clubs and activities, sports and so many new people to meet. I'm sort of a shy person, but there are a couple school clubs I'm interested in joining. I realize that when I participate in some fun or interesting activities, I actually enjoy school more. That helps me stay motivated to be a better student. Should I have goals for my interests and activities, too?"

GURU BOB'S ANSWER:

Have some activity and interest goals, too!

"Absolutely, Jamal! Middle school is a time to branch out, meet new people and try new activities, clubs or sports! Make sure to set some goals for these too. Keeping a healthy balance between school work, sports and social activities is important because being physically fit, enjoying friends and pursuing your interests and hobbies reduces some of the other stresses you may feel about school. That helps you stay motivated to be an organized student. But remember, clubs, sports and social activities are fun, but school work is your top priority!"

How's your social life? What are your interests? Do you want to try out for the basketball team? Join a school club? Write for the school newspaper? Try out for the play? What kinds of clubs, sports or after school activities are available at your middle school? Name ten, then circle three activities that are of interest to you. Make a plan to check out at least two of them.

1.

2.

3.

4.

5.

6.

7.

8.

9.

10.

My plan for checking out two of these activities:

_____

_____

_____

CHEAT

Stuck on the Level Four Challenge? Here's a cheat: There are teams, clubs and activities for all sorts of interests at nearly every middle school. Check your school's website or just ask around—you'll find one that interests you. Go to a meeting. Try out! If you're shy, ask a friend to go with you. Give the club, sport or activity a try for a couple of months. You'll know whether it's right for you. If you have an interest which is not represented by a school club or activity, check the school rules about forming a club.

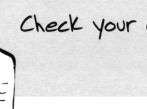

Check your answers on page 173.

YOU MAY ADVANCE TO LEVEL FIVE ➜

Third Stop: Motivation Mountain

Level 5 Challenge:

"In elementary school, I received rewards for spelling. Sometimes my teacher would put a star on my paper. Once I got a certificate for good conduct. That helped me stay motivated to do well in school. What kind of rewards will I get in middle school for good grades or good conduct?"

GURU BOB'S ANSWER:

"In middle school, achieving goals has rewards, but not stickers or stars like in elementary school. You are growing up, so rewards come more often in the form of good feelings such as pride, self-confidence and happiness. Don't overlook the value of these 'good feeling' rewards! They are far more valuable than any trophy or trinket. A 'good feeling' reward is like money in the Bank of Success! Cha-ching! Don't expect your parents to buy you a new pair of sneakers or reward you with money whenever you achieve one of your middle school goals. Sure, it's nice, but the best reward is their pride in you and in your accomplishments. You'll soon outgrow the sneakers, but the memory of a good feeling reward will stay with you forever. Learning to appreciate the value of good feeling rewards is important, because feeling good about yourself, and taking pride in your work, motivates you to stay organized and do well in school!"

The Middle School Student's Guide to Ruling the World!

BANK OF SUCCESS

Make a deposit in your Bank of Success! Here are some good feeling rewards that you can earn in middle school. Draw a line connecting the reward to the correct definition. Circle two rewards that you would most like to earn in middle school.

Reward	Definition
Happiness	
	Not influenced or determined by someone or something else; self-reliant.
Self-confidence	
	Enjoyment displayed or characterized by pleasure or joy.
Pride	
	The quality or state of mind or spirit enabling one to face danger or hardship with confidence or resolution.
Independence	
	Confidence in oneself or one's abilities.
Courage	
	Pleasure or satisfaction taken in one's work, achievements or possessions.

CHEAT

Stuck on the Level Five Challenge? Here's a cheat: These words can be found in a dictionary. If you don't know their meanings, look them up!

Check your answers on page 174.

YOU MAY ADVANCE TO LEVEL SIX ➜

Level 6 Challenge:

"I'm not sure what a 'goalbuster' is, but it doesn't sound good. It sounds like something that could defeat my goals. Like, I've been working really hard in history this semester because I want to improve my grade. I'm motivated! But, last week I couldn't resist watching just one more episode of Zorca the Zombie Orca. After that, I talked too long on the phone with friends. That left me with too little time to study for my history quiz and I got a low score. That hurt my goal!"

How is a goalbuster like Kryptonite?

GURU BOB'S ANSWER:

"Larry, do you know that there was just one substance in the universe that could defeat Superman? It was a fictional crystal called Kryptonite. Whenever Superman was in the presence of Kryptonite,

What's your Kryptonite?

he became weak and powerless and couldn't do anything. Fortunately, because he was keenly aware of his weakness, he was able to avoid Kryptonite, before it destroyed him.

"Most middle school students have habits or activities that, unless avoided or controlled, can overcome them and destroy their quest to achieve their goals—just like Kryptonite! They are 'goalbusters.' Knowing what your goalbusters are is the first step to controlling and avoiding them. Some activities, like using drugs, drinking alcohol or hanging with kids who do these or other stupid things are the worst of all goalbusters and must always be avoided! For others, it may be the timing that is the problem. Watching TV and talking on the phone with friends are not bad things. Everyone needs to relax. But the fact that you did these things before you studied for your quiz made them goalbusters for you. Well, now you know! Unless you have finished your homework and studying, avoid the TV and the phone like Kryptonite!"

The Middle School Student's Guide to Ruling the World!

1. Why was Kryptonite so dangerous for Superman?

2. How was Superman able to overcome the paralyzing power of Kryptonite?

3. All middle school students have certain habits or activities that, like Kryptonite, can defeat the achievement of their goals. What can be done by students to prevent the habit or activity from defeating their goals?

4. What goalbuster activities must *always* be avoided?

5. Some habits and activities are not necessarily bad. What is it that sometimes makes a habit or activity a "goalbuster"?

CHEAT

Stuck on the Level Seven Challenge? Here's a cheat: Reread page _____.

Check your answers on page 174.

YOU MAY ADVANCE TO LEVEL SEVEN →

Level 7 Challenge:

What's with the Attitude?

"I don't like math. I'm not good at math. My math teacher picks on me. I want to do well, but I've gotten mostly low scores on tests and quizzes. I'll probably *never* get a good grade in the class! My dad says one reason I don't do well in the class is because I have a bad attitude. I say attitude has nothing to do with it—I'm just not good at math!"

GURU BOB'S ANSWER:

"Chris, don't overlook the impact your attitude can have on reaching your goals! A negative attitude is a powerful goalbuster. A negative attitude drains you of energy and motivation. That leads to more negativity. On the other hand, a positive attitude actually generates energy! That helps you stay motivated to achieve, and helps you focus on learning, instead of focusing on your negative feelings. So, even if you don't care much for a subject, or you think you're not good at it, do your best to maintain a positive attitude. Maybe you'll never get an *A* in the class, but a positive attitude can make the difference between passing and failing a class. So, Chris, your dad is right. Watch your attitude, dude!"

> A positive attitude is a renewable energy source!

The Middle School Student's Guide to Ruling the World!

Find out if your attitude is negatively (–) or positively (+) charged! Think about a class or subject that is hard for you or that you dislike. Mark (–) if you've ever said or thought this about the class. Mark (+) if you haven't.

___ 1. "I don't like this class. It is sooooo boring!"

___ 2. "My teacher picks on me."

___ 3. "I'm the dumbest kid in this class."

___ 4. "I just want to pass this class and get out of here."

___ 5. "I don't have time to do extra credit."

___ 6. "I would understand this subject if the teacher were a better at teaching it."

___ 7. "I'm never going to need to know any of this stuff when I grow up, so why should I bother to learn it now?"

___ 8. "It's ok if I'm late to class. I never know what the teacher is talking about anyway."

___ 9. "Wake me up when class is over."

___ 10. "That teacher is about as exciting as watching paint dry."

CHEAT

Stuck on the Level Seven Challenge? Most students have a class that they don't much care for. Do you? Perhaps you don't like the teacher, maybe you don't like the subject. Your attitude about the subject or teacher may be causing you to not do as well as you should in class. So, try a change of attitude. It can't hurt!

Check your answers on page 174.

YOU MAY ADVANCE TO LEVEL EIGHT ➜

Here's how I put it all together

The Final Challenge – Can you put it all together?

"First I set my middle school grade goals by listing each of my classes and deciding what grade I can achieve by making my best effort in the class. I remembered the Goaldilock's Rule and set goals that are 'juuust right' for me: challenging, but within my reach! Then, I listed a couple of clubs and activities that I want to check out in middle school. I want to review video games for the school newspaper and join the journalism club.

"Next, I identified my personal goalbusters—those habits and activities that could defeat my goals. Like, I totally have a negative attitude in my writing class. Now that I know my negative attitude can hurt my grade, I am going to try to have a more positive attitude. I am making sure that I finish my homework and studying in time to watch my favorite show.

"I posted my Goal List at my workspace where I can see it. It helps me stay motivated to work hard in school and to keep up my new organizational skills. You know, Guru Bob, I totally rock!"

Good job, Larry, you do indeed uh... "rock."

MAKING A GOAL LIST

- Use the Goal List on page 167.
- List each of the classes you are taking in school.
- List the grade that you would expect to receive for making your best effort.
- List your personal goalbusters—the habits and activities which, if not controlled or avoided by you, can defeat your goals.
- Make a plan for controlling your goalbusters.
- Post your Goal List at your workspace, to help you stay motivated to achieve in middle school.

My Middle School Goals by _____

GRADE GOALS

Class: My Best Effort Grade Goal:

_____   _____

_____   _____

_____   _____

_____   _____

_____   _____

ACTIVITY AND INTEREST GOALS

Some Activity and Interest Goals I will pursue in middle school:

_____

_____

_____

GOALBUSTERS

My Personal Goalbusters:

1. _____   3. _____

2. _____   4. _____

My plan for avoiding or controlling my Goalbusters:

_____

_____

_____

YOU MAY ADVANCE TO THE TOP OF MOTIVATION MOUNTAIN!

Certificate of Ruling the World!

CONGRATULATIONS!

THIS IS TO CERTIFY THAT _____

(print your name here)

HAS COMPLETED THE LESSONS AND ACTIVITIES IN

THE MIDDLE SCHOOL STUDENT'S GUIDE TO RULING THE WORLD!

AND IS AN ORGANIZED AND TOTALLY AWESOME

MIDDLE SCHOOL STUDENT!

Answer Key

Pages 32 and 33

1. d; **2.** d; **3.** c; **4.** d; **5.** c; **6.** d; **7.** a; **8.** b; **9.** a; **10.** b

Page 47

					Sat/Sun Study for Monday's Math qz.
Monday Math qz chs 4&5	**Tuesday** Perm. Slip due; Rm 131 @3:00 Band practice: 3-5	**Wednesday** Due in Hist: R&O/L pp.223-240	**Thursday** Science: Rpt & vocab cards due.	**Friday** 11:00 Ortho appt. 3:30 BB Game	**Sat/Sun** Dad's Birthday!

Page 61

1. a; **2.** b; **3.** c; **4.** d; **5.** 8 (minutes); **6.** d; **7.** So that group members know what they need to accomplish and they stay on task.; **8.** d; **9.** d; **10.** c

Page 69

1. prepared; persistent; polite
2. yourself
3. polite
4. persistent; argumentative
5. final
6. following up
7. practice
8. listen in class; participate in class; say "thanks!"; apologize.
9. recheck
10. succeed

Page 79

"Good afternoon class. Will everyone please settle down? We have a lot to do today. Just a reminder, the Chapter 5 test is this Friday. It will consist of twenty multiple choice questions and five short answers. Bring two no. 2 sharpened pencils to class that day, as well as your 1812 Map handout. Okay class, today we're continuing with the topic of the War of 1812. Oh, one more reminder, please return all library books by Wednesday! If your book is not returned by Wednesday, I will take 2 points off of your test score. Also, please make sure that, no later than next Wednesday, you have selected the subject for your biographical report. Submit the name of the historical character to me on a lined 3x5 index card. The card must include the name and the birth date of the character and a reason why you have selected that person. One of you asked me whether Homer Simpson may be considered an important American historical figure. The answer is no. Now, continuing with our lesson. Today there are two things I want you to understand about the War of 1812. First, it is the war that made America a power on the international stage. Secondly, the War of 1812 opened the old Northwest to settlement..."

1. The War of 1812
2. (1) the war made America an international power and (2) the war opened the "old Northwest" to settlement.
3. Name, birthdate of character and the reason why you selected that person.
4. Return library book and turn in the biography card.
5. Two points will be deducted from your test score.

Page 96

The Rubric requires:	Describe how Jamal failed to follow directions:
Each of the graphics or photos is labeled to identify 1) the food pictured and 2) the food group to which the food belongs.	Jamal failed to properly label all of the pictures. Food group labels are missing for lasagna, milk and strawberries. The food label is missing for the salad.
A description of three safety procedures.	He only provided one safety procedure.
Two 3x5 unlined index cards identifying the name of a book on nutrition for teens, including title, author, publisher and number of pages.	He used lined index cards and failed to include the name of the author and the publisher of the book he selected.
Poster is neat and legible.	Although the poster is legible, it is not neat. His pictures and graphics are ragged looking and have not been neatly assembled on the posterboard. He has crossed out an error aboave his lab notes and the corner of his lab notes is torn. His printing is sloppy.
Contains student's name, date and class period in the lower right corner.	Jamal's name is in the lower left corner. He failed to include the date and the class period.

The Middle School Student's Guide to Ruling the World!

Page 105

1. Email and instant message study buds and group project members; Email your teacher.

2. Use your computer's word processing tools to insert page numbers, symbols, pictures and clip art, charts, diagrams and shapes into your reports and essays.

3. Use your computer's word processing tools to vary font styles and sizes, create paragraphs, bullet points and numbering, borders, shading and document styles.

4. Use your computer's word processing tools to check your spelling; use its thesaurus to improve your vocabulary on reports and essays.

5. Save time by using your computer's word count function.

6. Create a table or graph for reports and journals.

7. Use the Internet to research any topic, locate tutorials and find help for any homework problem.

8. Access your teacher's homepage for posted homework schedules, calendars, assignments, forms, grades, links and tutorials, email and office hours.

9. Access your school's policies and rules, annual schedule, parent organization information, links, newsletter, announcements, administrator and counselor's email, daily bulletin and campus map.

10. Access Information on student activities such as games, clubs, dances and community service; library, and health services and cafeteria menus.

Extra credit: After you check out your middle school website, go to www.middleschoolguide.com for tips on organizing for middle school, to access PDF forms and for other fun activities!

Page 115

There are many ways to give this essay an extreme makeover. Any makeover should include corrections of all spelling errors, correction of punctuation, selection of a better vocabulary and correction of grammatical errors. Here's one possible "AFTER" version:

There are many varieties of writing. There are nonfiction and fiction, including science, historical and realistic fiction. A well-written fiction story compels its readers. Ancient writing, including histories penned by Plato and Aristotle, reveals to the modern reader much about life and civilizations in the ancient world. Science fiction, such as many of the stories written by Ray Bradbury, often envisions how life will be in the future.

Page 138

Here's a "Split and Tackle Plan" Sara could use to finish her Long Term Project on time:

Monday 10	Tuesday 11	Wednesday 12	Thursday 13	Friday 14	Sat/Sun 15/16
Read/Review Project Instructions. Make list of supplies. Write plan in planner!	Begin research of New Deal Programs.	Complete research of New Deal Programs. Make notes and select a program.	Write essay draft.		Continue writing essay.
Monday 17	Tuesday 18	Wednesday 19	Thursday 20	**Friday 21**	Sat/Sun 22/23
Final draft and edit essay. Do word count.	Design and sketch poster.	Color poster. Make notes for speech.	Practice speech.	Social Studies Project Due!	

Here's a "Chunk and Block Plan" Sara could use to finish her Long Term Project on time:

Monday 10	Tuesday 11	Wednesday 12	Thursday 13	Friday 14	Sat/Sun 15/16
Read/Review Project Instructions. Make list of supplies. Write plan in planner!		After school: Research New Deal Programs at library. Select a program for essay; Collect notes on program.			Write essay (draft and final). Do word count.
Monday 17	Tuesday 18	Wednesday 19	Thursday 20	**Friday 21**	Sat/Sun 22/23
	Design, sketch and color poster.		Make speech notes; Practice speech.	Social Studies Project Due!	

Don't forget your supply list: Colored pencils and markers, 11"x17" poster board, and 3"x5" index cards!

Page 153

Level One Challenge
If you were able to identify a goal, and any effort you made toward achievement of your goal, you have demonstrated mastery of Level One.

The Middle School Student's Guide to Ruling the World!

Page 155

Level Two Challenge
There are far more than ten things you can do to make your best effort in a class! Any ten of these will do to demonstrate mastery of Level 2:

Organize your binder and keep it organized throughout the school year; clutter-bust your binder and locker; get a study bud in each of your classes and keep his/her 411 info handy; take "to do" and "to know" notes in class; use your planner consistently; participate in class; follow up on matters that affect your grade; take responsibility for your mistakes; ask a teacher for help when you need it; check your school's website often, and use your computer for homework help; make your Mental Checklist a daily habit; use the "write stuff" when writing essays and papers; create a productive work space; make a Homework Tracking Chart if you need one; do extra credit when it is offered; keep your rear in the chair when you do homework; use a Group Project Organizer for group projects; follow the Rules of Rubric Road; make a plan for Long Term Projects as soon as they're assigned...

Page 157

Level Three Challenge
1. patience; time
2. fail; lose confidence
3. low
4. doing what you already know what you are capable of doing
5. high; low; juuust right!

Page 159

Level Four Challenge
Check your middle school's website and ask around. Most middle schools will have a variety of sports programs—football, volleyball, soccer, baseball, lacrosse, track, cheerleading, dance, tennis, gymnastics, wrestling, swimming, water polo, etc. There are lots of sports programs that don't even require tryouts. Consider getting involved in a sport, for the health benefits and for fun. Check out some clubs for pursuing interests, such as journalism, politics, world affairs and languages, farming, 4-H, etc.

Page 161

Level Five Challenge

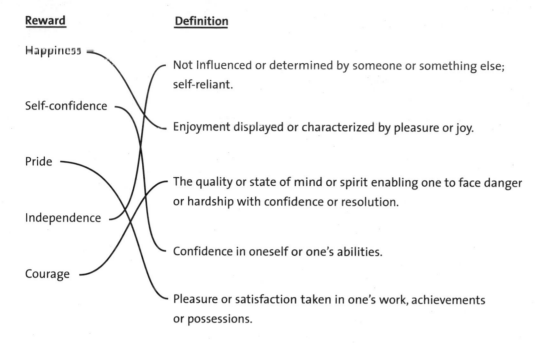

Reward	Definition

Happiness

Self-confidence

Pride

Independence

Courage

Not Influenced or determined by someone or something else; self-reliant.

Enjoyment displayed or characterized by pleasure or joy.

The quality or state of mind or spirit enabling one to face danger or hardship with confidence or resolution.

Confidence in oneself or one's abilities.

Pleasure or satisfaction taken in one's work, achievements or possessions.

Page 163

Level Six Challenge
1. Whenever Superman was in the presence of Kryptonite, he became weak and powerless.
2. He was keenly aware of Kryptonite's effect and avoided it at all times.
3. Know what your bad habits and weaknesses are and avoid them like Kryptonite!
4. Using drugs, drinking alcohol or hanging out with kids who do these or other stupid things.
5. Timing! Doing things like talking on the phone or watching t.v. <u>before</u> finishing homework, studying or completing projects.

Page 165

How many negative (–) signs did you mark?

8–10 = Uh-oh! Watch that negative attitude. It's bringing you down!

6–7 = Look out! You're getting heading into a negative zone.

5 = Neutral. Hmmm... you could go positive or negative, so watch your attitude!

3–4 = Looking pretty positive and it's showing!

0–1 = So positively charged! You're super!

The Middle School Student's Guide to Ruling the World!